Street by Street

C000213553

PLYMOUTH

PLYMPTON, SALTASH, TORPOINT, WEMBURY

Brixton, Cawsand, Cremyll, Heybrook Bay, Kingsand, Millbrook, Plymstock, Rame, Roborough, Tamerton Foliot

3rd edition October 2006
© Automobile Association Developments Limited 2006

Original edition printed May 2001

Ordnance Survey® This product includes map data licensed from Ordnance Survey® with the permission of the Controller of Her Majesty's Stationery Office. © Crown copyright 2006. All rights reserved. Licence number 399221.

Published by AA Publishing (a trading name of Automobile Association Developments Limited, whose registered office is Fanum House, Basing View, Basingstoke, Hampshire RG21 4EA. Registered number 1878835).

Mapping produced by the Mapping Services Department of The Automobile Association. (A02659)

A CIP Catalogue record for this book is available from the British Library.

Printed by Oriental Press in Dubai

The contents of this atlas are believed to be correct at the time of the latest revision. However, the publishers cannot be held responsible or liable for any loss or damage occasioned to any person acting or refraining from action as a result of any use or reliance on any material in this atlas, nor for any errors, omissions or changes in such material. This does not affect your statutory rights. The publishers would welcome information to correct any errors or omissions and to keep this atlas up to date. Please write to Publishing, The Automobile Association, Fanum House (FH12), Basing View, Basingstoke, Hampshire, RG21 4EA. E-mail: streetbystreet@theaa.com

Ref: ML110y

Key to map pages	ii-iii
Key to map symbols	iv-1
Enlarged map pages	2-3
Main map pages	4-39
Index – towns & villages	40
Index – streets	40-46
Index – featured places	47
Acknowledgements	48

ii

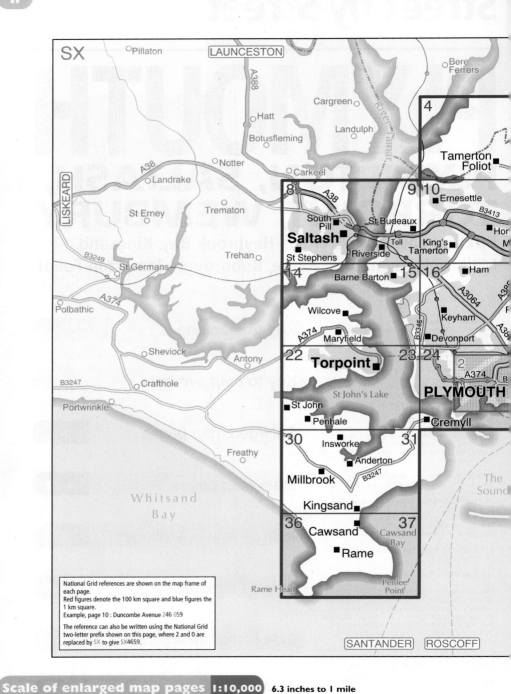

SX

Pillaton

LAUNCESTON

Bere Ferrers

Cargreen

Hatt

Landulph

4

Botusfleming

Tamerton Foliot

Notter

Carkeel

A38

LISKEARD

Landrake

8

A38

9 10

Ernesettle

B3413

St Erney

Trematon

South Pill

St Budeaux

Hor

Saltash

Toll

King's Tamerton

M

Trehan

Riverside

St Germans

St Stephens

14

15

16

Ham

Barne Barton

A3064

A3

Polbathic

A374

Wilcove

B3346

Keyham

A36

Maryfield

Devonport

A374

Sheviock

22

Torpoint

23 24

2

A374

B

Antony

PLYMOUTH

B3247

Crafthole

St John's Lake

St John

Cremyll

Portwrinkle

Penhale

30

31

Freathy

Insworke

The Sound

Anderton

B3247

Whitsand

Millbrook

Bay

Kingsand

36

37

Cawsand

Cawsand Bay

Rame

Rame Head

Penlee Point

National Grid references are shown on the map frame of each page.
Red figures denote the 100 km square and blue figures the 1 km square.
Example, page 10 : Duncombe Avenue 246 059

The reference can also be written using the National Grid two-letter prefix shown on this page, where 2 and 0 are replaced by SX to give SX4659.

SANTANDER   ROSCOFF

Scale of enlarged map pages 1:10,000   6.3 inches to 1 mile

| 0 | | 1/4 | | miles | | 1/2 |
| 0 | 1/4 | | 1/2 | kilometres | 3/4 | 1 |

TAVISTOCK

A386

Shaugh Prior

DARTMOOR
NATIONAL
PARK

Wotter
Lee Moor

Bickleigh **7**

Roborough

Woolwell

Glenholt

Cornwood

Lutton

Plymouth **13**

B3432

erriford

Estover

wnhill

Mainstone

Sparkwell

Eggbuckland **19**

Hemerdon

Longbridge

Plympton

B3416

Underwood

B3416

Chaddlewood

Venton

Lee Mill

EXETER

Ivybridge

A38

rd

A374

A38

B3214

20   **21**

Mount Gould **27 28**   **29**

TORBAY

Westlake

A3121

Billacombe

A379

Oreston

Plymstock

Elburton

Worston

Yealmbridge

A379

chapel

Hooe

34

Combe

35

Brixton

Yealmpton

Dunstone

Staddiscombe

Spriddlestone

Holbeton

33

39

Down
omas

Knighton

Heybrook
Bay

WEMBURY

B3186

Newton
Ferrers

Bridgend

Noss Mayo

Mothecombe

Wembury
Bay

Gara
Point

SX

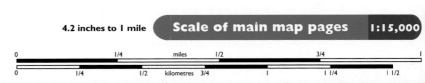

4.2 inches to 1 mile   **Scale of main map pages**   1:15,000

| 0 | 1/4 | miles 1/2 | 3/4 | 1 |
| 0 | 1/4 | 1/2 | kilometres 3/4 | 1 | 1 1/4 | 1 1/2 |

Junction 9	Motorway & junction
Services	Motorway service area
	Primary road single/dual carriageway
Services	Primary road service area
	A road single/dual carriageway
	B road single/dual carriageway
	Other road single/dual carriageway
	Minor/private road, access may be restricted
← ←	One-way street
	Pedestrian area
	Track or footpath
	Road under construction
	Road tunnel
P	Parking
P+	Park & Ride
	Bus/coach station
	Railway & main railway station
	Railway & minor railway station
⊖	Underground station
⊖	Light railway & station
+++++++++	Preserved private railway

LC	Level crossing
●—●—●—●	Tramway
- - - - - - -	Ferry route
....	Airport runway
— · — · — · —	County, administrative boundary
▼▼▼▼▼▼▼▼	Mounds
17	Page continuation 1:15,000
3	Page continuation to enlarged scale 1:10,000
	River/canal, lake, pier
	Aqueduct, lock, weir
465 ▲ Winter Hill	Peak (with height in metres)
	Beach
	Woodland
	Park
	Cemetery
	Built-up area
	Industrial/business building
	Leisure building
	Retail building
	Other building

⊓⊓⊓⊓⊓⊓	City wall	♞	Castle
A&E	Hospital with 24-hour A&E department	⌷	Historic house or building
PO	Post Office	Wakehurst Place NT	National Trust property
📖	Public library	Ⓜ	Museum or art gallery
i	Tourist Information Centre	♣	Roman antiquity
i	Seasonal Tourist Information Centre	⚱	Ancient site, battlefield or monument
▮▮	Petrol station, 24 hour Major suppliers only	▂▂	Industrial interest
†	Church/chapel	❋	Garden
🚻	Public toilets	◉	Garden Centre Garden Centre Association Member
♿	Toilet with disabled facilities	❀	Garden Centre Wyevale Garden Centre
PH	Public house AA recommended	🌳	Arboretum
🍴	Restaurant AA inspected	🛒	Farm or animal centre
Madeira Hotel	Hotel AA inspected	🦌	Zoological or wildlife collection
🎭	Theatre or performing arts centre	🦜	Bird collection
🎥	Cinema	🐋	Nature reserve
⚑	Golf course	🐟	Aquarium
▲	Camping AA inspected	V	Visitor or heritage centre
🚐	Caravan site AA inspected	⍦	Country park
▲🚐	Camping & caravan site AA inspected	⌒	Cave
🎢	Theme park	🌾	Windmill
⛪	Abbey, cathedral or priory	🛢	Distillery, brewery or vineyard

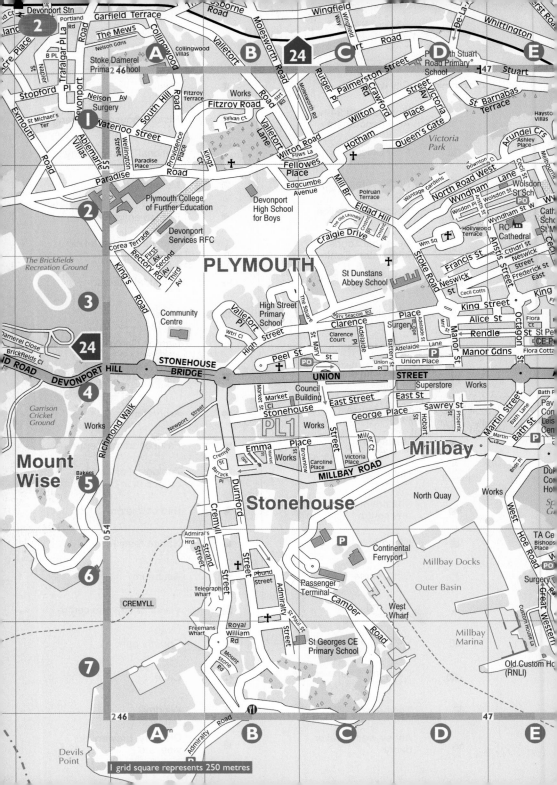

4

A   B   C   D

245   63   46   Bl

1

New Barn
Farm

River Tavy

2

62

3

Warren   Lane

Old Warleigh   Lane

Tavy
Bridge

Tamert
Foliot

4

Old   Warleigh   Lane

Fo
Str
Nu

190

Riverside
Walk

5

Lake View
Close

Devon County
City of Plymouth

Station Road

Tamerton
Close

245   46

A   B   **10**   C   D

Holly Park
Close

Holly Park Drive

Lakeview Drive

Milford

Northampton Close

Lane

bury Crescent

Lakeside   Drive

Manston
Avenue   Avenue

Gv

Stapleford
Gardens

Cmbm Cl
R C

Norwi

New

Hereford
Road

Brentford Rd

1 grid square represents 500 metres

Bame Wood

E   F   G   H

48   49   63

Broadley

Blaxton

Peter Hopper's Hill

I

Blaxton Lane

Ashleigh Barton

Horsham

Ashleigh Lane

2

Allern Lane

Porsham

62

Roborough Lane

3

Braggs Farm

Porsham Lane

Devon County City of Plymouth

6

Cunningham Road

Linton Close

Gresham Close

Deans Prim Sch

Henley Dr

Ashleigh Cl

Dean Av

Whitsoncross Lane

Coombe Lane

Downham Gardens

Coombe Lane

Wills Close

Winnicott Cl

Kinnaird

Crescent

Lizard Cl

Langley Close

Langley Cres

Cromer Close

Bardsey Cl

Clittaf

4

Clittaford Road

Flambor Road

Waring Road

Moses Close

Leatherby Cl

Lundy Cl

Pentland

Clittaford

Alderney Road

Inchkeith Road

PO

Harwood Avenue

Dunnet Road

Godding Gdns

Rdclf Cl

Burnard Cl

Srpl Cl

Skerries Road

Rockfield Avenue

Southway Drive

Longstone Aven

Goodwin Aven

Rockhill

Surg

Hancock Cl

Billing Cl

Petrick Cl

Hurrell Close

Main

Southway Primary School

Southway Community College

Bond Street

Clittaford Rd

Way

Pendeen Close

Pendee

5

Cresce

Church Row Lane

Foliot Road

Tamerton Vale Primary School

Blackmore

Jeffery Cl

Crs

Hornbrook Gdn

Cann Cotts

Bampfylde

Hendwell Close

Bampfylde Way

Southway

TAMERTON FOLIOT ROAD

Rolston Cl

Cheshire Dr

Hutchings

Bonville Road

Middlefield Road

Bampfylde Way

573

E   F   II   G   H

48   49

William Evans Close

Frontfield Crescent

Copleston Rd

The Arbour

Southway Drive

Upland Drive

Dunraven

Moorla

Powisland

Borrowdale Close

Looseleigh

Warleigh Crescent

Looseleigh Park

Mistew Cl

Lopwell Close

Tretower Cl

Notre Dame RC School

Woodfield Primary

E   F   G   H
52   53
63

Little Down Lane

Upperton Lane

Hele Lane

Hele

Plym Valley Path and Cycle Route

I

Bickleigh

Ham
Farm

Bickleigh
Vale

Hele Cl

Hitchill Farm

New Road

2

62

3

Hedgerow
Close

Rockwood
Road

Drive

Church

Park Road

N.W.Cl

Clove Rise

Campion Vw

Violet Cl

Churchlands Rd

Spring Pk

Churchlands
Close

Bowers Pk Dr

Coppers
Park

Cann Wood View

Pinewood Drive

Roseland Way Dr

Mulberry
Cl

Birch Cl

Larch Dr

Maple Way

River Plym

Plym Valley Path and Cycle Route

4

61

5

Jasmine
Gdns

Glenfield Wy

Maple Cl

Kingfisher
Close

mt Wk

Laurel Drive

Devon County
City of Plymouth

Great Shaugh Wood

E   F   G   H

Darklake Cl

View

Darklake

13

52   53

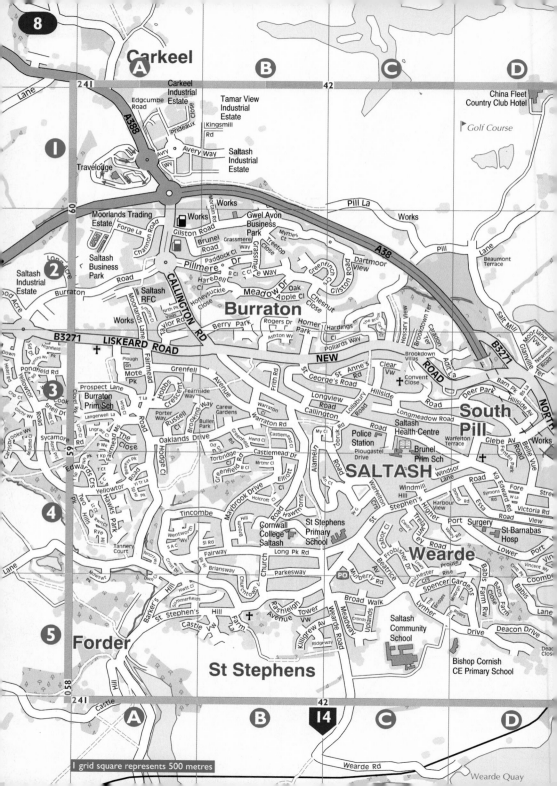

Skinham
Point

E F G H

44 45

Devon County
City of Plymouth

Warren
Works

Cornwall County
City of Plymouth

Lakeside
Manston Clo
here Avenue
I
North Wld Gdn Catterick Cl
Duxford
Northolt Av
Hornchurch
Rd
Uxbridge
Chivenor Av
Exeter Cl
Debden Cl Maidstone
Rd
Croydon
2 Hawkinge

Ernesettle Lane

River Tamar

Works

Northolt Av

Ernesettle

Ernesettle Lane

Yelvertor
Close

St Budeaux

Agaton Rd
Victoria Road

3

10

Ferry

Tamar
Bridge

THE PARKWAY

TAMAR BR

Toll

Saltash
Station

Mary Newman's
Cottage
Tamar
Terrace

Fore St
Silver St
Tamar St

Bickham Rd

Victoria Road
Verna Pl
Vera Rd
Peter's
Chard Rd
Mount Tamar
Special
School
Roman
Park
Lane

4

Waverley
Rd

Admiralty
Rd

Normandy

Way

Normandy Hl

Vicarage
Gdns

Pemros
Road

Wolseley
Road

Ltl Ash Gdns

Little Ash Rd

Works

Riverside

Stanhope Rd
Walters
Birgwn
Lghbr
Rd
Tenby Rd
Loftus
Gardens
Saltburn Rd
Seacroft Rd
Ivanhoe Rd
Evelyn St
Stirling Road
Lynher St
Kathleaven St
Florence
St
Collin Cl
Sunny Dene
St Pauls RC
Primary School
Victoria Road
Edith St
Percy
St Victoria Road
Primary School
Shelley Av
Wakefield Av
Clearbrook Av
Colebrook Rd

5

Moor Lane

Road

Fegan Rd
Bull Point
Primary School

Warburton
Gdns
Foulston
Reynolds
Haydon
sithney
Rennie
Wolseley Road
St Budeaux
Victoria Rd.Stn
Trelawney
Av
Fletemoor

Cardinal
Avenue
Church Way

PO

E F 15 G H

44 45

Bull
Point

Landrake
Cl
St Budeaux Ferry
Road Station
Barne Barton
Primary School

Kinterbury Road

Police
Stn
Poole Park Rd
Kit Hill Crs
Old Farm
Roberts Road

A   **B**   **4**   **C**   **D**

Walk

Lake View Close

Devon Co
City of Plymouth

245

46

1

Lakeside Drive

Tangmere Avenue
Manston Close
Digby Gv
Avenue
Stapleford Gardens
Rochford
Crescent
Holly Park Close
Holly Park Drive
Lakeview Drive
Milford
Northampton Close
Aylesbury Cresc
Hereford Road
Brentford
Newcastle Garden

North Wld Gdn
Catterick Cl
Duxford
Hornchurch Rd
Malling Av
Hh La
Ernesettle Gn
Lympne Avenue
Biggin Hill
Maltby St
Surgery
Drive
Kenley Gdns
Russet Wd
Truro Drive
Norwich Avenue
Winchester Gdns
Cmbrn Cl
R C
Okm Rd
Milford Lane
PL5
Woo Spe Scho
Westbury

2
Northolt Av
Exeter Cl
Trevanor Rd
Grosvenor Cl
Maidstone Pl
Uxbridge
Croydon Gdns
Hawkinge
Gardens
Middleton Wk
Redhill Close
Ackorum
St Eval Pl
Martlesham Pl
Ernesettle Infant School
Mill Ford Special School
Coltishall Close
Budshead Road
Ringmore Way
Canterbury Dr
Hills Spe Scho
Budshead Road

Ernesettle
Yelverton Close
Crlrs
Perranporth Close
Ernesettle Lane
Marina Road
Queens Road
Kings Road
Jubilee Rd
Parade Rd
Anzac Av
Valiant
Rs
Knowle Primary School
Ringmore Way
Belstone Close
Cheriton Close
Princess Av
Sheldon Crs
Lmrtn

3
Ernesettle Crs
Council Building
B3413
Marett
Dunstone Rd
Chatsworth Gdns
Wollaton Gv
Hirmandale Rd
Sterford Crs
PO
B3413 **CROWNHILL ROAD**
Council Building
Ashburnham Road
Surg
Honicknowle Gn
Chard Barton
Warwick Orchard Cl

9

59

Agaton Rd
Victoria Road
Roman Way
Priestley Av
Pistw
St Budeaux Foundation Junior School
Plaistow Hill Infant School
Cayley
Teignmouth Rd
Coombe Park Lane
Duncombe Avenue
Eastbury Avenue
Wanstead Gv
West Park Primary School
Little Ashridge Gdns
Dock Lane
Medical Cen

4
Bickham Rd
Victor
Verna Pl
Surgery
Chard Road
Row
Lane
Roman Road
Mount Tamar Special School
Rorkes Cl
Newton Av
Cayley
Ho Cl
Hrgrvs
Nw Gs
A38
L D L
Montacute Avenue
Stowe Gdns
Harewood Crs
Honicknowle Lane

Lynher St
Evelyn St
Kathleaven St
Collin Cl
Peters
Park Lane
Wakeham
Ferrers Rd
Peters Pk
Cleatbrook Rd
Trevithick Rd
Weston Mill Road
King's Tamerton Road
Tamarside Community College
Flamsteed Crs
Coombe Wy
Mowhay Road
Weston Mill Lane
Burrington Industrial Estate
Walkham Business Park
Rmny Cl

King's Tamerton

5
St Victoria Road Primary School
Fletemoor
Borrington Av
245
Cardinal Avenue
Moor Lane
Weston Mill Hill
Weston Mill
Adams Cl
A3064
Mowhay Road
Burrington Road
Burrington Way
The John Kitto Community College

A   **B**   **16**   **C**   **D**

Church Road
Jackson Close
Tucker Cl
North
Abbotsbury Wy
Cleeve Gardens
Ham
Dryburgh
Malmesbury Cl

46

Careswell Av

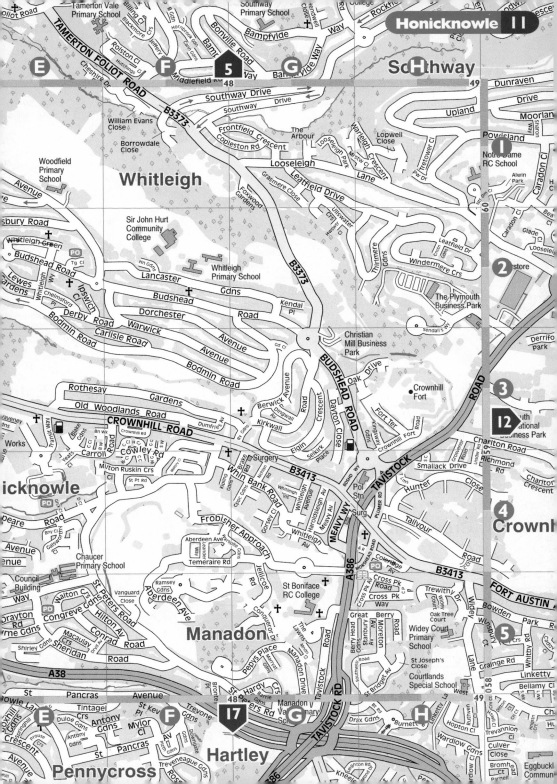

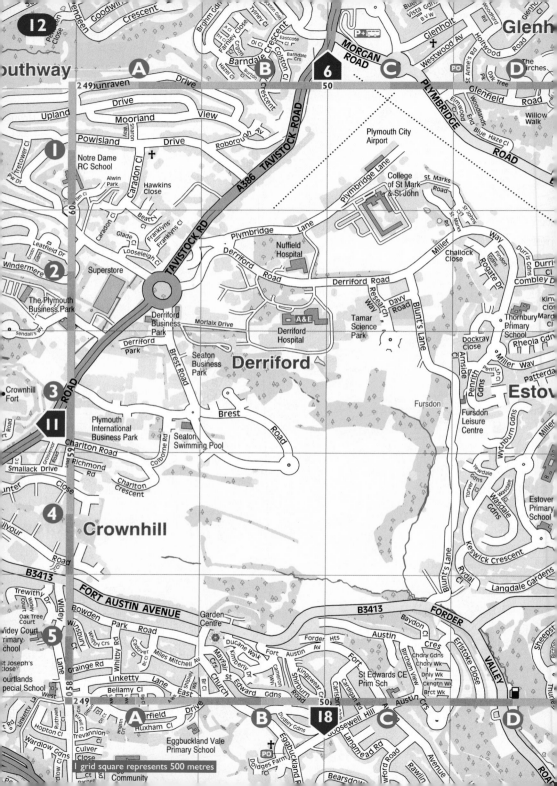

Jasmine Gdns
Glenfield Wy
Maple Cl
Kingfisher Close

E

Devon County
City of Plymouth

F

7
52

Great Shaugh Wood

G

H

53

I

Darklake Cl
View

Darklake

60

Industrial Estate

Estover Cl

Estover Cl

Estover Road

B3432

Thornbury Road

Estover Industrial Estate

Works

Phoenix Business Park

2

Plym Valley Path and Cycle Route

Burwell

Yardley Gdns

Wm Pl
Wk Pl
Westwood Gdns
Wy Pl

Way

Industrial Estate

River Plym

3

59

Long Down Gdns

Ashdown

Plymbridge Road

Bush Park

Pendlesham Gdns

Road

Colwill Road

Earls Wd Dr

Earls Wd Cl

Ramage Cl

Hatshill Cl

Wood Park

NOVOROSSISK ROAD

Leypark Walk

Chelson Gdns

Weir Road

Towers Cl

Pethill

Cl

Hurrabrook Gdns

stover
alth Centre

rive

Briarleigh Cl

Weir Cl

Weir Gdns

4

PO
Leypark WK

Pattinson Drive

Pattinson

B3432

Mainstone

Cressbrook Dr

Plym Brown

Plymbridge Road

Plymbridge Road

er Way

Hallerton Cl

Parkfield Drive

Woodlands La

Plym Valley Path and Cycle Route

City of Plymouth

Devon County

5

Bampton Rd

Bradfield Close

Beechwood Rise

Parkfield Drive

ham
ary
ool

Cockington

Shell Cl

Luxmore close

Millwood Drive

58

ostor Rd

Mthcmb Wk

chrchstw

Grimspound Cl

LeighFam

E

19
52

G

H

53

Torbryan Cl

Babba

Bgbry Wk

Brxhm Wk

Leigha

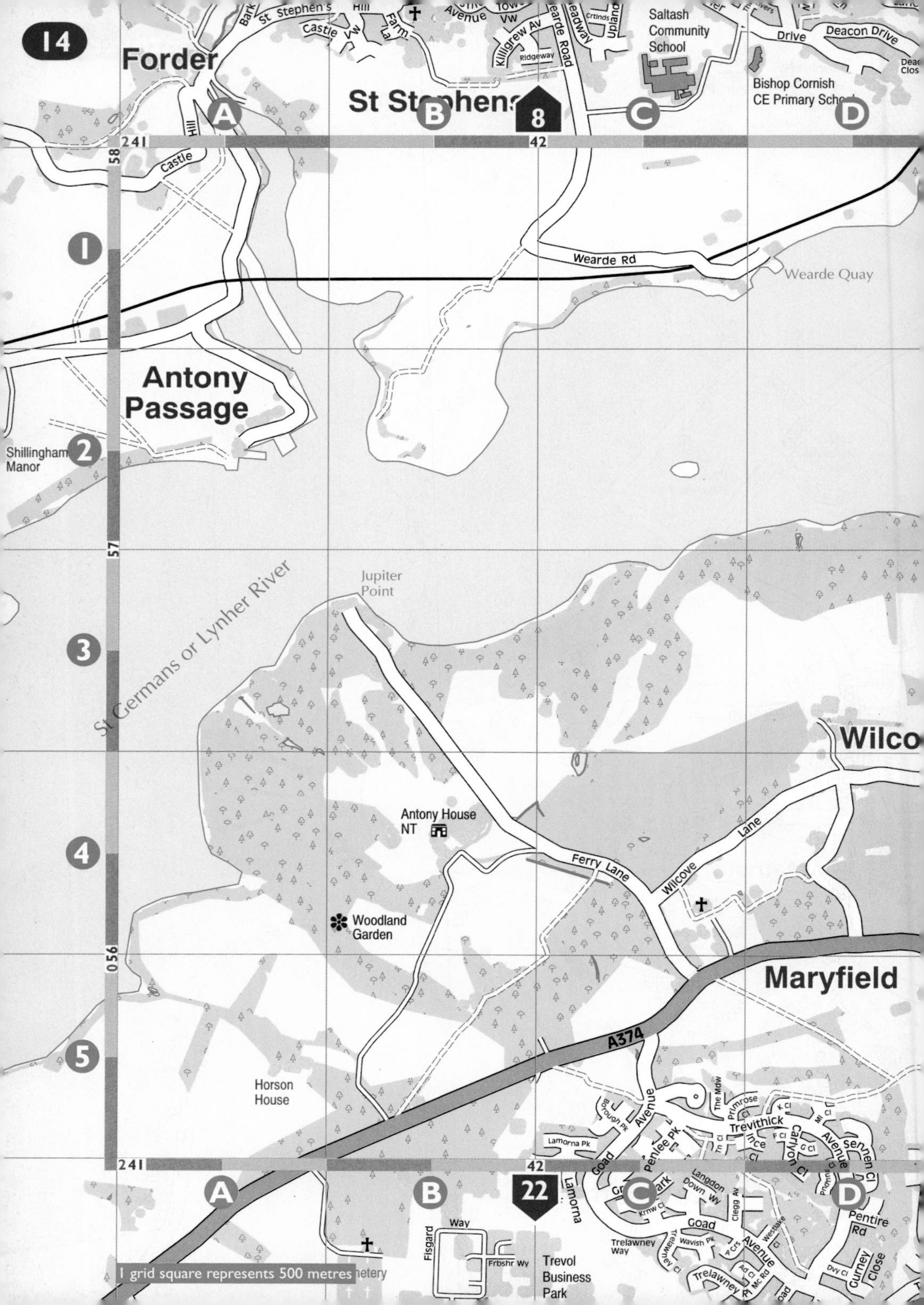

14

Forder

St Stephens

Saltash
Community
School

Bishop Cornish
CE Primary School

St Stephen's
Hill
Castle Vw
Farm
Avenue
Killigrew Av
Ridgeway
Wearde Road
Upland
Deacon Drive
Drive
Deac
Clos

A **B** **8** **C** **D**

241 42

58 241

1

Castle Hill

Wearde Rd

Wearde Quay

Antony
Passage

2

Shillingham
Manor

57

St Germans or Lynher River

Jupiter
Point

3

Wilco

Antony House
NT

Ferry Lane

Wilcove

Lane

4

Woodland
Garden

056

Maryfield

5

Horson
House

A374

Trevithick

The Maw
Primrose
Avenue
Caryyol Cl
Goad
Avenue
senen Cl
Lamorna Pk
Pentee Pk
Langadon
Down Wy
Clegg Av
Pentire
Rd

241 42

A **B** **22** **C** **D**

Fisgard
Way

Frbshr Wy

Trevol
Business
Park

Lamorna
Goad
Trelawney
Way
Wavish Cl
Trelawney Av
Gurney
Close

Pentire
Rd

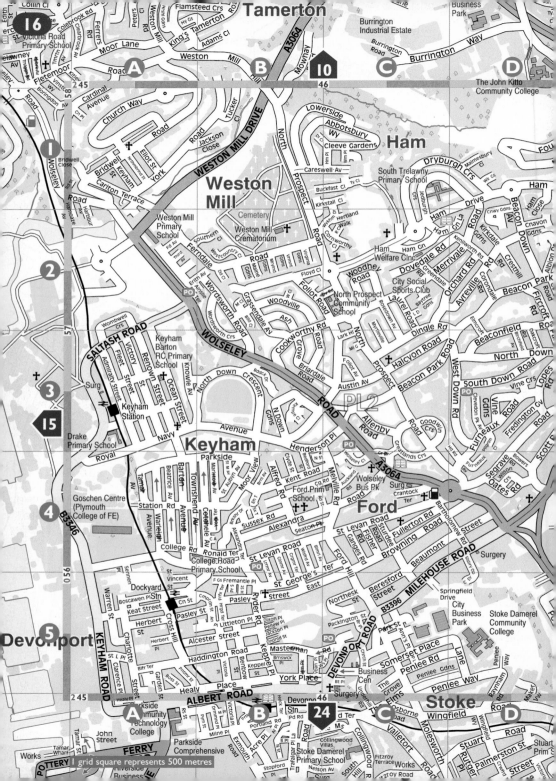

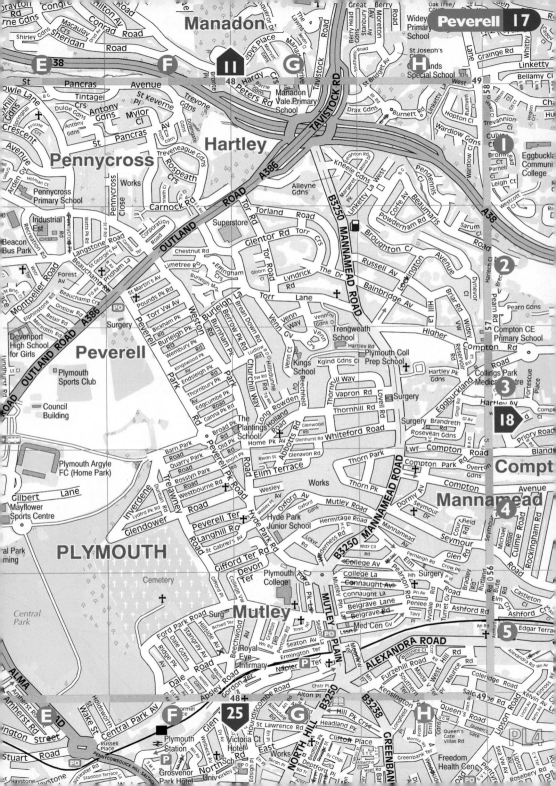

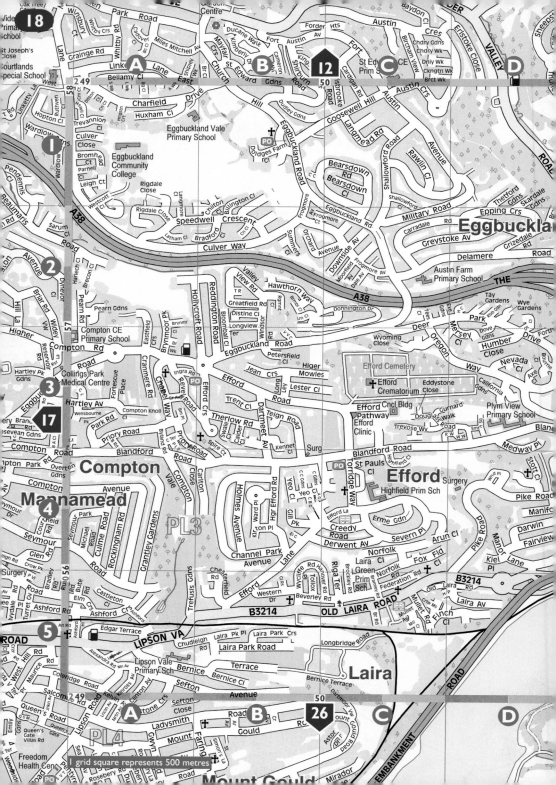

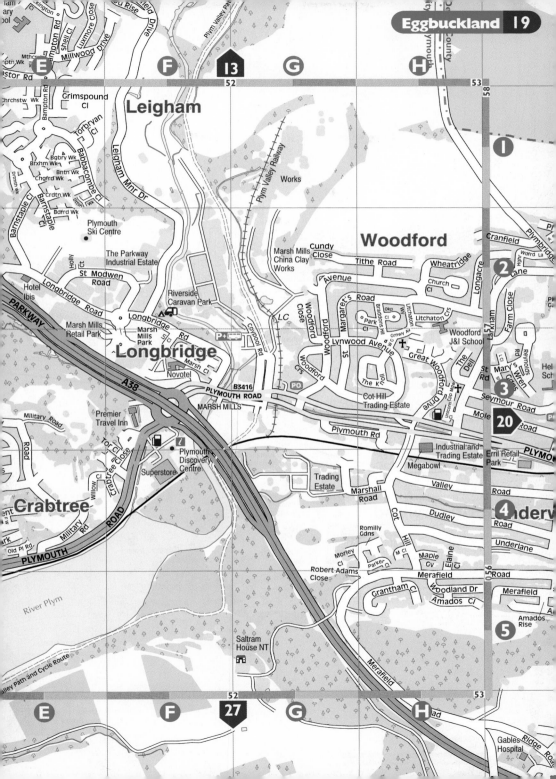

E · F · **13** · G · H

52 · 53 · 58

I

Leigham

Grimspound Cl

Torbryan Cl

Babbacombe La

Bgbry Wk
Brxhm Wk
Chgfrd Wk
Bntn Wk
Crdtn Wk
Drmth Wk

Leigham Mnr Dr

Barnstaple Cl
Barnstaple
Bdfrd Wk

Plymouth Ski Centre

The Parkway Industrial Estate

St Modwen Road

Hotel Ibis

Longbridge Road

Marsh Mills Retail Park

Marsh Mills Park

Longbridge

Longbridge Rd

Marsh Cl

Novotel

PARKWAY

A38

Military Road

Premier Travel Inn

Tor Cl

Crabtree Close

Willow Cl

Crabtree

Old Pl Rd

PLYMOUTH

Military Rd

ROAD

PLYMOUTH ROAD
B3416
MARSH MILLS

Superstore

Plymouth Discovery Centre

Plym Valley Railway

Works

Riverside Caravan Park

Longbridge

P+

Coypool Rd

LC

Woodford

Cundy Close
Marsh Mills China Clay Works

Tithe Road

Wheatridge

Church Cl

Longacre

Avenue

St Margaret's Road

Woodford Close

Litchaton Crs

Litchaton

Brad:ons Hill

Okpk

Park Cl

Grnwy Av

Woodford J&I School

Woodford Crs

Lynwood Avenue

Great Woodford Drive

St Mary's Cl

Reynolds Rd

Wren Cl

The Dell

Cranfield

Plymbridge

Wdfrd La

Farm Close

Laskham

2

3

St Mary's Rd

Mole Rd

20

Seymour Road

PLYMO

PO

Cot Hill Trading Estate

Unicorn Spt Mdw

The K Cl

Plymouth Rd

Industrial and Trading Estate

Erril Retail Park

Megabowl

Trading Estate

Marshall Road

Cot Hill

Valley

Dudley

Road

Road

Romilly Gdns

Morley Cl

Robert Adams Close

Parker

M Cl

Maple Gv

Elaine

Merafield

Woodland Dr

Amados Cl

Amados Rise

Grantham

Merafield

4

nderv

Underlane Road

056

5

River Plym

lley Path and Cycle Route

Saltram House NT

Merafield Road

E · F · **27** · G · H

52 · 53

Gables Ridge Hospital

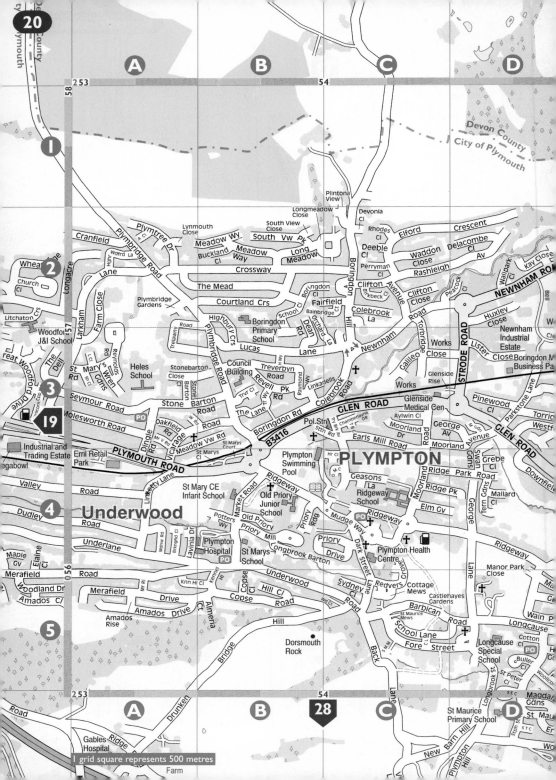

Lobb Farm

E   F   G   H

56   57   58

Works

Newnham Park

1

B3417

Hemerdon Lane

Calva Road

Hemerdon

Newnham Road

West Park Hill

2

Newnham Cl
Compass Drive
Furzeacre Cl
Bridle Close
Cornfield Gdns
Hangman Dr

Newnham Industrial Estate

57

Highglen Dr

ugy Lane

Greenwood Pk Cl
Greenwood Cl
Liddle Wy   Wild Cl

Chaddlewood

3

Hemerdon Hts
Almond Dr
Park Road
Raleigh Ct
Gilbert Ct
Grenville Ct
Clurvd Ct
Glennaven Close
Ashwood Pk Rd

Kingston
Litchfield
Wint Cl
Ashwood Drive
Aspen Gdns
Wallingham Ct
Steer

Kingston Cl
Redwood Drive
Poplar
Hickory Wy
Fern
Barton
Down
Park Road
Barnfield Drive

Chaddlewood J&I School
Bedford
Nash
Glen Park Prim Sch
Rowan
Juniper
Periwinkle
Western Wood Way
Beechwood Way

B3416
GLEN
PO
Hickory Dr
Horswell
Tillard
Road
Holland
4

Hillcrest Close
Deveron Cl
Foxle
Woirige Av
Woirige Way
Clement Rd
Surgery
Eastern Wood Road
Langage Industrial Estate

Wensum Cl
Hillcrest Drive
Robyns Cl
Moulton Cl
Edwards Drive
Crd
Totnes Cl
Kirkwelly
Rowdown Close
Garden Close

Longwood Close The Spinney
Edwards Cl
Sparke Close
Pode Dr
Bellingham Crs
Dunster
Eagle Rd
Meadow Close

aggon Hill
New Pk Rd
Wallace Rd
Cornwood Road
Maurice View
B3416 SANDY ROAD
Ashleigh Way
Langage
Barn Close
5

Yeomans Way
Meadow Rise
Yeampstone
Maddock Drive
Ridgeway
56

Lwr Farm Rd
Maddock Cl
Colliford Cl
Brimhill Cl
Neal Cl
Yeampstone Dr

57

E   F   **29**   G   H

Broadlands
Brook Close
Yealmstone Farm Primary School
Lotherton Cl
Hasest Cl
Higher Pk Cl

Cherry Tree La
Aycliffe Cl
Aycliffe Gdns
Mdwfld Pl
Canefields Avenue

Burniston Cl
Canhay Cl
Greenlees
irelands Cl
LANE

A38

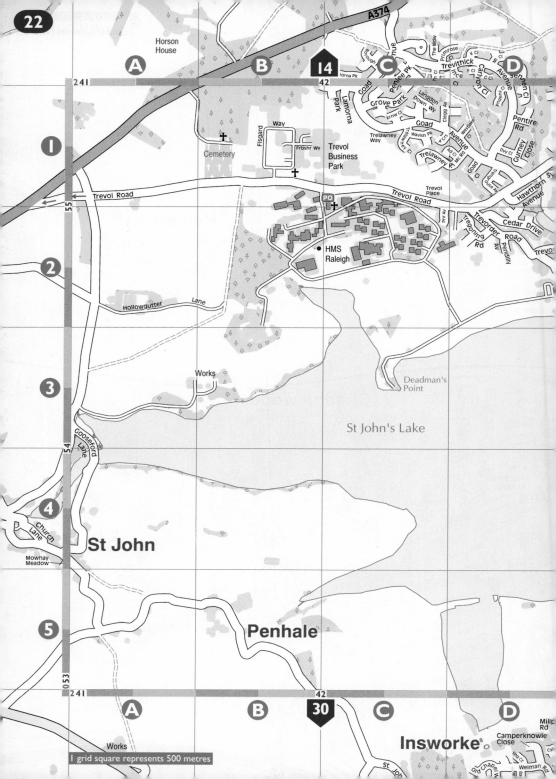

Devonport

E
The
wns
Thanckes Lake
F
15
44
G
ty of Plymouth
Cornwall Count
H
45
YHAM ROAD
St L Pl
Charlotte
Clarence Pl
Healy Pl

ANTONY ROAD

Torpoint
Infant Sch
Rd
Sydney
Rd
Adela Rd
Clarence
Road
Albion
Well Pk Rd
Gravesend
Road
Albion
Court

Racquets
Sports Club
Gv Gs
PO
MCt

Pa
Go
Tec
Col

John
Street

TORPOINT

Evenden
Court
arbeile
nior
school

Khyber
Cl
Beech
Av
Cl Rd
Mill Lane
Milnouse
Park
Carbeile
Peacock
Roselaire Av
Jago
Av
Scobier
Rd
Buller Rd
York Road
Moor Vw
B Rd
Roberts Av
Wellington St
Salamanca St
P Rd
Vct St
VCE St
kmotn ter

Surg
Works
Quarry St
Wesley
Court

FORE ST
HARVEY ST

Police
Station

Works
Tamar
Wharf
POTTERY RD

New Pd
Riverside
Business
Park

FER
RO

I

Chapeldown Road
Maker
Road
North
Kingsley Av
Liscawn
Ter
St James Rd
Vicarage
Rd
Cremyll Rd
Hamoaze Road
Marine Dr
Barossa Road
Ba Rd
Ferry St
A374

Fire
Station

Arthur
Terrace

Carew Wharf
Business Centre

Hamoaze
Place
H M
Dockyard
Cannon St
Cornwall St
Holmans Buildings

Queen
Morice St
St
Surg
St Aubyn
W Cl
WN Cl

Granby

Marlborough
Prim Sch

PO

2

55

54

Devonport Guildh
Eh St
Duke
St
Mount W
Primary
James

3

24

Mutto

4

go
d

Southdown

Works

P

5

Empacombe
B3247
53
45

E

FGrt Cl
inswrk
sthvw
South
Down
Terrace
Silver
Terrace

F
44

31

G

H

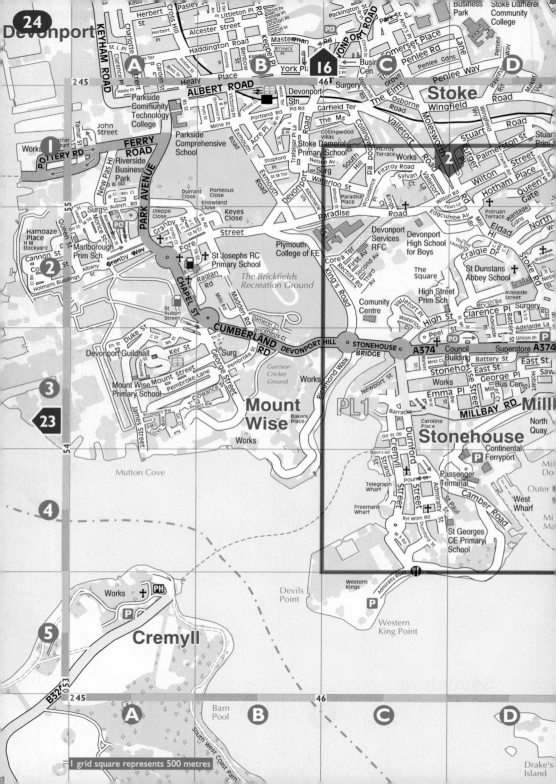

30

Penhale

A B **22** C D

241 42

53

1 Works

Insworke

Mill Rd

Camperknowle Close

St John's Rd

Trefusis Terrace

snd Ct

Weiman Barton Mews

Old Chapel Way

Clinton Terrace

Blindwell Hill

St John's Ct

Newport Street

B3247

Millbrook CE Primary School

Molesworth Terrace

Priesthood Terrace

Mount Pleasant

Greenland

Lower

Higher

Anderton

Mill View Rd

speedwell

Anderton Road

2

Lane

52

La New St

Fore St

PO

Kng St

Knill Cross

Maker

And

St Andrew Street

West St

West St

Millpool Head

Hounster Dr

HOUNSTER HILL

WEST ST

West

P

Dodbrook

Anderton Lane

Tregonhawke

Radford Lane

Millbrook

B3247

3

Farm

Whitsand Bay Holiday Park

Donkey Lane

Treninnow

4

PL10

051

Wiggle

5

South West Coast Path

Military Road

Trencher Lane

Hat Lane

241 42

A B **36** C D

Forder Hill

K

Forder

1 grid square represents 500 metres

E **Southdown** F 23 G H

Empacombe

B3247

South Down Terrace

Silver Terrace

Road

I

P

Millbrook Lake

Mount Edgcumbe House & Country Park

2

P

B3247

MAKER LANE

3

Maker Heights

Maker Farm

South We

...nesend County ...ry School

Drive

4

...oombe Farm

Earl's

New Road

...ckman's

The

South West Coast Path

...and

Coombe Park

Meadow

Close

New Rd Close

New Road

Cawsand Bay

5

Fore St

Kngswy

The Cleave

PO

PH

44 37 G H

E The Fort

New Road St Andrew's St

F

P Kiln Cl

Armada Road

St Andrew's Pl

The Earl

...and

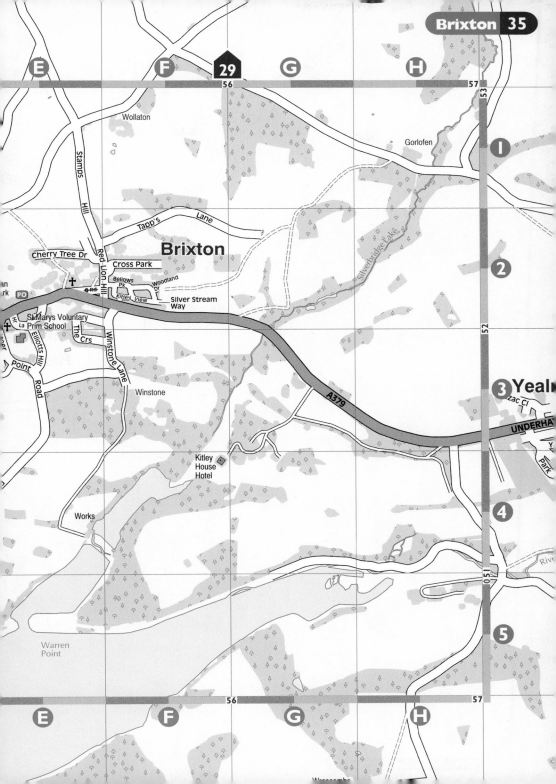

E F **29** G H

56 57

Wollaton

Gorlofen

I

Stamps Hill

Tapp's Lane

Silverbridge Lake

Brixton

Cherry Tree Dr

Cross Park

Bellows Pk

Woodland Dr

Red Lion Hill

2

Kitley View

Silver Stream Way

PO

St Marys Voluntary Prim School

The Crs

Elliotts Hill

52

Point Road

Winstone Lane

Winstone

A379

3 Yeal

Zac Cl

UNDERHA

Park

Kitley House Hotel

4

Works

051

River

Warren Point

5

E F G H

56 57

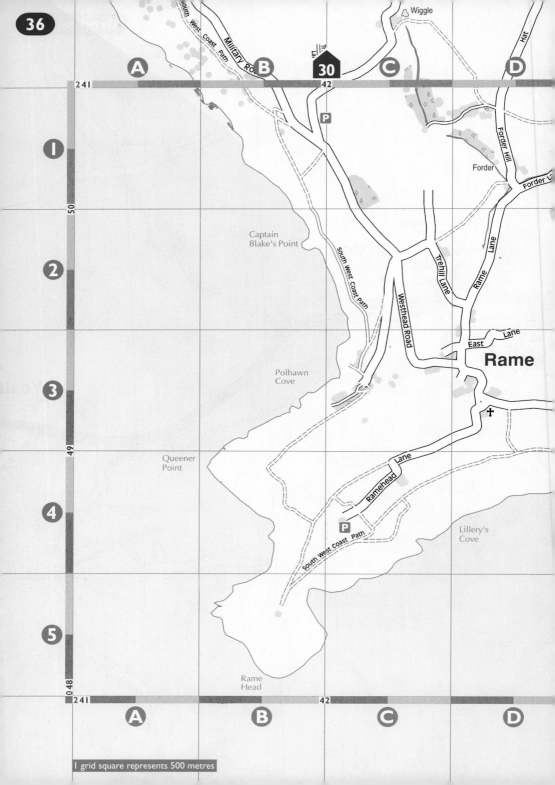

241

A B 30 C D

42

1

50

Wiggle

Hat

Military Ro...

South West Coast Path

Tre
La...

P

Captain
Blake's Point

2

Forder Hill

Forder

Forder L...

South West Coast Path

Trehill Lane

Rame Lane

Westhead Road

East Lane

Polhawn
Cove

3

Rame

✝

49

Queener
Point

Ramehead Lane

4

P

Lillery's
Cove

South West Coast Path

5

Rame
Head

048

241

A B C D

42

1 grid square represents 500 metres

Cawsand Bay

E **F** **31** **G** **H**

I

2

3

4

5

New Rd
Close
New Rd
Fore St
The Cleave
PO
PH
The Fort
New Road
St Andrew's St
Kiln Cl
Armada Road
St Andrew's Pl
The Earl's Dr
Garrett Street
Pier La
MrK's

and**E**

wsand

St Andrew's Pl

The Earl's Drive

ry Road

P

South West Coast Path

The Earl's Drive

Penlee
Point

44 45

50

49

048

44 45

E **F** **G** **H**

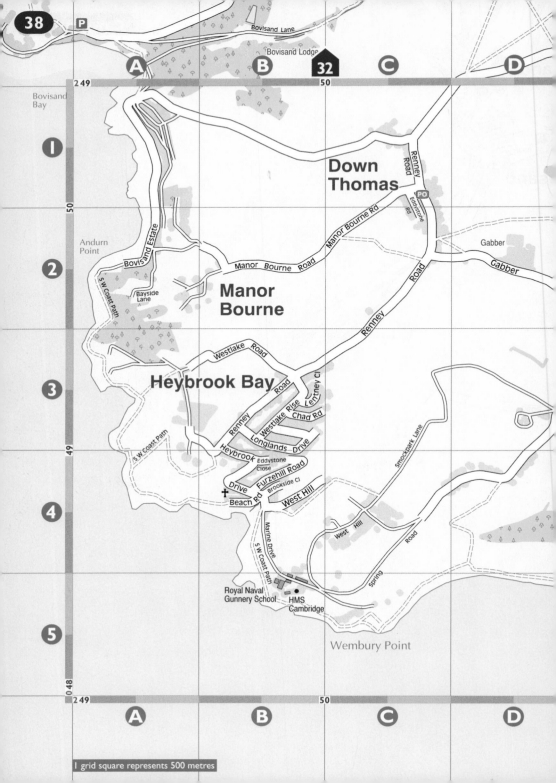

Hollacombe
Hill

E **F** **33** **G** **H**

52

Hollacombe Brake

Traine Road

Wembury Road

I

50

Raneleigh
Farm

Adam's Lane

Langdon
Court Hotel

Knighton

Knighton

Priory Court

2

Upland
Gdns

Knighton Hill
Business
Centre

Ford Road

PO

Highfield Dr

Wembury
Mdw

Barton Cl

Wembury
Primary
School

Ryeland Cl

Leyford Cl

3

49

Low Rd

Erme Pym Trail

High Road

Middle Rd

Church Walk

Cross Pk

Valley Dr

Crawys

Crawys

Collier's Close

Rd

Mewstone Avenue

Brownhill Lane

Beach Vw

Southland Crs

Park Crs

Southland Pk

Hillcrest Cl

Sea Vw

Dr

Librnm Dr

Surgery

Vpk

Vw

Veasypark

WEMBURY

Southland Crs

Rose Park

Hawthorn Park Road

Warren

St Werburgh Close

Hawthorn Dr

Church Road

Warren La

4

Cliff Road

P

Marine
Centre

South West Coast Path

N Barton

5

048

The Old Mill
NT

E **F** **G** **H**

52 53

Wembury Bay

Season Point

Anderton	30 D3	Devonport	15 H5
Antony Passage	14 A2	Down Thomas	38 C1
Barbican	3 H5	Efford	18 C4
Barne Barton	15 G1	Eggbuckland	18 D2
Bickleigh	7 G1	Eilburton	28 B5
Billacombe	27 F4	Ernesettle	9 H2
Brixton	35 F2	Estover	12 D3
Broadley	6 A1	Ford	16 C4
Burraton	8 B2	Forder	8 A5
Cattedown	25 H4	Glenholt	6 D5
Cawsand	36 D1	Ham	16 C1
Chaddlewood	21 F3	Hartley	17 F1
Combe	34 D2	Hemerdon	21 G2
Compton	18 A4	Heybrook Bay	38 A3
Crabtree	19 E4	Hollacombe Hill	33 H5
Cremyll	24 A5	Honicknowle	10 D4
Crownhill	12 A4	Hooe	32 C2
Derriford	12 B3	Insworke	30 C1

Keyham	16 A3	Oreston	26 C4
Kingsand	30 D5	Penhale	22 B5
King's Tamerton	10 B5	Pennycross	17 E1
Knighton	39 G2	Peverell	17 E3
Laira	18 C5	Plymouth	2 A3
Langage	21 H1	Plympton	21 E5
Leigham	19 F1	Plymstock	27 E5
Longbridge	19 F3	Pomphlett	27 E5
Mainstone	13 E4	Rame	36 D3
Manadon	11 F5	Riverside	9 F5
Mannamead	17 H4	Roborough	6 D2
Manor Bourne	38 B2	St Budeaux	9 G4
Maryfield	14 D5	St John	22 A4
Millbay	2 D5	St Stephens	8 B5
Millbrook	30 C3	Saltash	8 C5
Mount Gould	26 B1	Southdown	23 E5
Mount Wise	24 B3	South Pill	8 D5
Mutley	17 F5	Southway	5 H5

Spriddlestone	34
Staddiscombe	33
Stoke	24
Stonehouse	2
Tamerton Foliot	4
Torpoint	23
Turnchapel	26
Underwood	20
Wearde	8
Wembury	39
Weston Mill	16
Whitleigh	11
Widewell	6
Wilcove	14
Woodford	19
Woolwell	6

USING THE STREET INDEX

Street names are listed alphabetically. Each street name is followed by its postal town or area locality, the Postcode District, the page number, and the reference to the square in which the name is found.

Standard index entries are shown as follows:

Abbotts Rd *EFF/MANN* PL3 .... **17** G4

Street names and selected addresses not shown on the map due to scale restrictions are shown in the index with an asterisk:

Alcester Cl *KEY/HAM/PCR* PL2 * .. **16** A5

GENERAL ABBREVIATIONS

ACC	ACCESS	CTYD	COURTYARD	HLS	HILLS	MWY	MOTORWAY
ALY	ALLEY	CUTT	CUTTINGS	HO	HOUSE	N	NORTH
AP	APPROACH	CV	COVE	HOL	HOLLOW	NE	NORTH EAST
AR	ARCADE	CYN	CANYON	HOSP	HOSPITAL	NW	NORTH WEST
ASS	ASSOCIATION	DEPT	DEPARTMENT	HRB	HARBOUR	O/P	OVERPASS
AV	AVENUE	DL	DALE	HTH	HEATH	OFF	OFFICE
BCH	BEACH	DM	DAM	HTS	HEIGHTS	ORCH	ORCHARD
BLDS	BUILDINGS	DR	DRIVE	HVN	HAVEN	OV	OVAL
BND	BEND	DRO	DROVE	HWY	HIGHWAY	PAL	PALACE
BNK	BANK	DRY	DRIVEWAY	IMP	IMPERIAL	PAS	PASSAGE
BR	BRIDGE	DWGS	DWELLINGS	IN	INLET	PAV	PAVILION
BRK	BROOK	E	EAST	IND EST	INDUSTRIAL ESTATE	PDE	PARADE
BTM	BOTTOM	EMB	EMBANKMENT	INF	INFIRMARY	PH	PUBLIC HOUSE
BUS	BUSINESS	EMBY	EMBASSY	INFO	INFORMATION	PK	PARK
BVD	BOULEVARD	ESP	ESPLANADE	INT	INTERCHANGE	PKWY	PARKWAY
BY	BYPASS	EST	ESTATE	IS	ISLAND	PL	PLACE
CATH	CATHEDRAL	EX	EXCHANGE	JCT	JUNCTION	PLN	PLAIN
CEM	CEMETERY	EXPY	EXPRESSWAY	JTY	JETTY	PLNS	PLAINS
CEN	CENTRE	EXT	EXTENSION	KG	KING	PLZ	PLAZA
CFT	CROFT	F/O	FLYOVER	KNL	KNOLL	POL	POLICE STATION
CH	CHURCH	FC	FOOTBALL CLUB	L	LAKE	PR	PRINCE
CHA	CHASE	FK	FORK	LA	LANE	PREC	PRECINCT
CHYD	CHURCHYARD	FLD	FIELD	LDG	LODGE	PREP	PREPARATORY
CIR	CIRCLE	FLDS	FIELDS	LGT	LIGHT	PRIM	PRIMARY
CIRC	CIRCUS	FLS	FALLS	LK	LOCK	PROM	PROMENADE
CL	CLOSE	FM	FARM	LKS	LAKES	PRINCE	PRINCESS
CLFS	CLIFFS	FT	FORT	LNDG	LANDING	PRT	PORT
CMP	CAMP	FTS	FLATS	LTL	LITTLE	PT	POINT
CNR	CORNER	FWY	FREEWAY	LWR	LOWER	PTH	PATH
CO	COUNTY	FY	FERRY	MAG	MAGISTRATE	PZ	PIAZZA
COLL	COLLEGE	GA	GATE	MAN	MANSIONS	QD	QUADRANT
COM	COMMON	GAL	GALLERY	MD	MEAD	QU	QUEEN
COMM	COMMISSION	GDN	GARDEN	MDW	MEADOWS	QY	QUAY
CON	CONVENT	GDNS	GARDENS	MEM	MEMORIAL	R	RIVER
COT	COTTAGE	GLD	GLADE	MKT	MARKET	RBT	ROUNDABOUT
COTS	COTTAGES	GLN	GLEN	MKTS	MARKETS	RD	ROAD
CP	CAPE	GN	GREEN	ML	MALL	RDG	RIDGE
CPS	COPSE	GND	GROUND	MNR	MANOR	REP	REPUBLIC
CR	CREEK	GRA	GRANGE	MS	MEWS	RES	RESERVOIR
CREM	CREMATORIUM	GRG	GARAGE	MSN	MISSION	RFC	RUGBY FOOTBALL CLUB
CRS	CRESCENT	GT	GREAT	MT	MOUNT	RI	RISE
CSWY	CAUSEWAY	GTWY	GATEWAY	MTN	MOUNTAIN	RP	RAMP
CT	COURT	GV	GROVE	MTS	MOUNTAINS	RW	ROW
CTRL	CENTRAL	HGR	HIGHER	MUS	MUSEUM	S	SOUTH
CTS	COURTS	HL	HILL			SCH	SCHOOL

SE	SOUTH EA...
SER	SERVICE AR...
SH	SHO...
SHOP	SHOPPI...
SKWY	SKYW...
SMT	SUMM...
SOC	SOCIE...
SP	SP...
SPR	SPRI...
SQ	SQUA...
ST	STRE...
STN	STATI...
STR	STREA...
STRD	STRA...
SW	SOUTH WE...
TDG	TRADI...
TER	TERRA...
THWY	THROUGHWA...
TNL	TUNN...
TOLL	TOLLWA...
TPK	TURNP...
TR	TRA...
TRL	TR...
TWR	TOW...
U/P	UNDERPA...
UNI	UNIVERSI...
UPR	UPPER...
V	VA...
VA	VALE...
VIAD	VIADU...
VIL	VIL...
VIS	VIS...
VLG	VILLA...
VLS	VIL...
VW	VIE...
W	WE...
WD	WO...
WHF	WHA...
WK	WA...
WKS	WAL...
WLS	WEL...
YD	YA...
YHA	YOUTH HOST...

POSTCODE TOWNS AND AREA ABBREVIATIONS

EFF/MANN	Efford/Mannamead	MBRK/KGSD	Millbrook/Kingsand	PLYMP	Plympton	PLYNW	Plymouth northwest	TOR	Torpo...
KEY/HAM/PCR	Keyham/Ham/Pennycross	PLY	Plymouth	PLYMST/WEM	Plymstock/Wembury	RPLY	Rural Plymouth	YLMP	Yealmpt...
		PLYE	Plymouth east	PLYNE	Plymouth northeast	SALT	Saltash		

A

Abbotsbury Wy	
KEY/HAM/PCR PL2	16 C1
Abbotts Rd EFF/MANN PL3	17 G4
Aberdeen Av PLYNW PL5	11 F5
Abingdon Rd PLYE PL4	6 A1
Abney Crs PLYNE PL6	6 B5
Acklington Pl PLYNW PL5	10 A2
Acre Pl PLY PL1	24 B1
Adams Cl PLYNW PL5	10 B5
TOR PL11	22 C1
Adams Crs TOR PL11	22 C1
Adam's La PLYMST/WEM PL9	39 E2
Addison Rd PLYE PL4	3 J1
Adelaide La PLY PL1	2 D4
Adelaide Pl PLY PL1	2 C3
Adelaide St KEY/HAM/PCR PL2	16 B4
Adelaide Street Ope PLY PL1	2 D5
Adela Rd TOR PL11	23 E1
Adit La SALT PL12	8 C3
Admiral's Hard PLY PL1	2 A6
Admiralty Rd PLY PL1	24 C5
PLYNW PL5	9 F4

Admiralty St KEY/HAM/PCR PL2	16 A3
PLY PL1	2 B6
Agaton Rd PLYNW PL5	10 A4
Ainslie Ter KEY/HAM/PCR PL2	16 A2
Aire Gdns EFF/MANN PL3	18 B4
Alameln Ct SALT PL12	8 B4
Alamein Rd SALT PL12	8 B4
Albany St PLY PL1	24 A2
Albemarle Vis PLY PL1	24 B1
Albertha Cl PLYE PL4	3 K1
Albert Rd KEY/HAM/PCR PL2	24 A1
SALT PL12	8 D4
Albion Ct TOR PL11	23 F1
Albion Dr KEY/HAM/PCR PL2	16 D2
Albion Rd TOR PL11	23 F1
Alcester Cl KEY/HAM/PCR PL2 *	16 A5
Alcester St KEY/HAM/PCR PL2	16 A5
Alderney Rd PLYNE PL6	5 H4
Aldersley Wk PLYNE PL6	18 A1
Alexandra Cl	
PLYMST/WEM PL9	27 H4
Alexandra Rd	
KEY/HAM/PCR PL2	16 B4
PLYE PL4	17 H5
PLYNE PL6	11 H4
Alexandra Sq SALT PL12	9 E4

Alexandra Ter	
KEY/HAM/PCR PL2	16 B4
Alfred Rd KEY/HAM/PCR PL2	16 B4
Alfred St PLY PL1	3 G5
Alice St PLY PL1	2 D3
Allenby Rd	
KEY/HAM/PCR PL2	16 C3
Allendale Rd PLYE PL4	25 C1
Allern La PLYNE PL6	5 F2
Alleyne Gdns EFF/MANN PL3	17 G1
Allhallows Rd PLYNE PL6	16 D5
Alma St PLYE PL4	25 H3
Almeria Ct PLYMP PL7	20 B5
Almond Dr PLYMP PL7	21 F3
Alton Pl PLYE PL4	25 C1
Alton Rd PLYE PL4	25 C1
Alvington St PLYE PL4	25 H3
Alwin Pk PLYNE PL6	12 A1
Amacre Dr PLYMST/WEM PL9	32 B1
Amados Cl PLYMP PL7	19 H5
Amados Dr PLYMP PL7	20 A5
Amados Ri PLYMP PL7	20 A5
Amherst Rd EFF/MANN PL3	25 E1
Amherst Road La East	
EFF/MANN PL3	17 E5
Amity Pl PLYE PL4	3 K1

Anderton Quay	
MBRK/KGSD PL10 *	30 D2
Anderton Ri MBRK/KGSD PL10	30 D2
Andurn Cl PLYMST/WEM PL9	33 H1
Ann's Pl EFF/MANN PL3	16 C5
Anson Pl KEY/HAM/PCR PL2	16 B5
PLYE PL4	25 H2
Anstis St PLY PL1	2 E2
Antony Gdns	
KEY/HAM/PCR PL2	17 E1
Antony Rd TOR PL11	15 E5
Anzac Av PLYNE PL6	10 C2
Apsley Rd PLYE PL4	25 F1
The Arbour PLYNE PL6	11 G1
Arcadia PLYMST/WEM PL9	34 B1
Arcadia Rd PLYMST/WEM PL9	34 A1
Archer Ter PLY PL1	3 F2
Archway Av PLYE PL4	26 B1
Arden Gv KEY/HAM/PCR PL2	17 E1
Ark Royal Cl PLYNW PL5	15 H1
Arley Cl PLYNE PL6	6 B5
Arlington Rd PLYE PL4	17 H5
Armada Rd MBRK/KGSD PL10	37 E1
Armada St PLYE PL4	3 H2
Armada Wy PLY PL1	3 G5
Armeen Cl PLYMST/WEM PL9	33 E2

Arnside Cl PLYNE PL6	12
Arscott Gdns PLYMST/WEM PL9	32
Arscott La PLYMST/WEM PL9	32
Arthur Ter TOR PL11	23
Artillery Pl PLYE PL4	25
Arun Cl EFF/MANN PL3	18
Arundel Crs PLY PL1	2
Arundel Ter	
KEY/HAM/PCR PL2 *	16
Ashburnham Rd PLYNW PL5	15
Ashcombe Cl PLYMP PL7	20
Ashdown Cl PLYNE PL6	5
Ashery Dr PLYMST/WEM PL9	33
Ashford Cl PLYE PL4	18
Ashford Crs PLYE PL4	18
Ashford Hl PLYE PL4	18
Ashford Rd PLYE PL4	18
Ash Gv KEY/HAM/PCR PL2	16
Ashleigh Cl PLYNW PL5	5
Ashleigh La PLYNE PL6	5
Ashleigh Wy PLYMP PL7	21
Ashley Pl PLY PL1	2
Ashridge Gdns PLYNW PL5	10
Ashton Cl PLYNE PL6	6
Ashton Ms SALT PL12 *	8
Ashton Wy SALT PL12 *	8

tree Cl PLYNE PL6......6 D4
wood Cl PLYNE PL7......21 F4
wood Park Rd PLYMP PL7......21 G3
en PLYMP PL7......21 G4
er Dr PLY PL1......26 C1
anaeum La PLY PL1......3 F4
anaeum St PLY PL1......3 F5
erton Pl
KEY/HAM/PCR PL2 *......16 A5
kland Rd
KEY/HAM/PCR PL2......16 C4
in Av KEY/HAM/PCR PL2......16 B5
in Crs PLYNE PL6......12 C5
ry Wy SALT PL12......8 A1
eville Rd PLYMP PL7......20 C3
eville Rd KEY/HAM/PCR PL2...16 D2

B

bacombe Cl PLYNE PL6......19 E1
is Farm Cl SALT PL12......8 D5
is Farm Rw SALT PL12......8 D4
is La SALT PL12......8 D5
k La SALT PL12......8 B4
k La PLYMP PL7......20 C5
ger Vw PLYMST/WEM PL9...32 D2
nbridge Av EFF/MANN PL3...17 H2
nbridge Ct PLYMP PL7......20 B2
ers Cl PLYMP PL7......21 G4
ers Pl PLY PL1......24 B3
our Ter KEY/HAM/PCR PL2...16 A5
Pk SALT PL12 *......8 B5
moral Av KEY/HAM/PCR PL2...16 B4
npylde Wy PLYNE PL6......13 C5
npton Rd PLYNE PL6......13 E5
bican Ap PLYE PL4......25 H3
bican Rd PLYMP PL7......20 C5
Barbican PLYE PL4......3 K5
bury Crs PLYE PL4......16 C5
cote Wk PLYNE PL6......12 C5
dsey Cl PLYNE PL6......6 A4
sing St PLYE PL4......25 H1
ker's Hl SALT PL12......8 A5
low Gdns
KEY/HAM/PCR PL7......16 D2
n Cl PLYMP PL7......21 H5
ndale Crs PLYNE PL6......15 C1
ne Cl PLYNW PL5......9 H5
ne La PLYNW PL5......15 C1
ne Rd PLYNW PL5......15 C1
nfield Dr PLYMP PL7......21 G4
ningham Gdns PLYNE PL6...6 A5
n Pk SALT PL12......8 D3
n Park Rd EFF/MANN PL3...17 H4
nstaple Cl PLYNE PL6......19 E2
nwood Cl PLYMST/WEM PL9...33 E2
ossa Rd TOR PL11......23 F2
rack PLY PL1......2 B5
rack St PLY PL1......24 A2
re Gdns PLYNW PL5......11 C5
tholomew Rd
KEY/HAM/PCR PL2......16 C4
ton Av KEY/HAM/PCR PL2...16 A4
ton Cl PLYMP PL7......21 G4
ton Ms MBRK/KGSD PL10...39 H2
ton Rd PLYMST/WEM PL9...26 B5
nkgatt Ope PLY PL1 *......33 E5
sket Ope PLY PL1......3 J5
ch La PLY PL1......2 E4
ch Pl PLY PL1......2 E4
ch Rd PLY PL1......2 E4
tershall Ct
PLYMST/WEM PL9......33 F2
ter St PLY PL4......3 J4
tery St PLY PL4......3 J4
inton Wk PLYNE PL6......19 E2
ydon Cl PLYNE PL6......12 C5
dry's Rd PLYMST/WEM PL9...26 B5
yside La PLYMST/WEM PL9...38 A2
yswater Rd PLY PL1......3 F1
ytree Gdns
KEY/HAM/PCR PL2......16 C2
ach Rd PLYMST/WEM PL9...38 B4
ach View Crs
PLYMST/WEM PL9......39 C3
acon Down Av
KEY/HAM/PCR PL2......16 D1
aconfield Rd
KEY/HAM/PCR PL2......16 D3
acon Park Rd
KEY/HAM/PCR PL2......16 C5
are Cl PLYMST/WEM PL9...32 B2
arsdown Cl PLYNE PL6......18 C1
arsdown Rd PLYNE PL6......18 C1
atrice Av KEY/HAM/PCR PL2...16 A4
PLYE PL4......25 H2
SALT PL12......8 C5
atrice Gdns SALT PL12 *......8 C5
attie Rd PLYNE PL6......15 F1
atty Cl PLYNE PL6......12 A2
auchamp Crs
KEY/HAM/PCR PL2......17 E2
auchamp Rd
KEY/HAM/PCR PL2......17 E2
auly Cl PLYMP PL7......21 E4
aumaris Gdns
EFF/MANN PL3......17 H1
aumaris Rd EFF/MANN PL3...17 H1
aumont Av PLYE PL4......3 K2
aumont Pl PLYE PL4......3 K3
aumont Rd PLYE PL4......25 H2
aumont St
KEY/HAM/PCR PL2......16 C4
aumont Ter SALT PL12......8 D2
ckford Cl PLYMP PL7......21 E4
ckham Pl EFF/MANN PL3...18 A3
de Gdns PLYNW PL5......11 E5

Bedford Pk PLYE PL4......3 K1
Bedford Park Vls PLYE PL4 *...25 C1
Bedford St PLYMST/WEM PL9...27 E4
Bedford St KEY/HAM/PCR PL2...16 B4
Bedford Ter PLYE PL4......3 J3
Beech Av PLYE PL4......26 A3
Beech Cl TOR PL11......23 E1
Beech Ct PLYNE PL6......12 D1
Beechcroft Rd EFF/MANN PL3...18 A5
KEY/HAM/PCR PL2......16 D2
Beechfield Gv KEY/HAM/PCR PL7...17 C5
Beechwood Av PLYE PL4......17 C5
Beechwood Ri PLYNE PL6......13 E5
Beechwood Ter PLYE PL4......17 F5
Beechwood Wy PLYNE PL6...21 H4
Belair Rd KEY/HAM/PCR PL2...17 F2
Belgrave La PLYE PL4......17 C5
Belgrave Rd PLYE PL4......17 C5
Bellamy Cl PLYNE PL6......12 A5
Bell Cl PLYMP PL7......20 D2
Belle Acre Cl EFF/MANN PL3...17 H4
Belle Vue Av PLYMST/WEM PL9...32 B2
Belle Vue Dr PLYMST/WEM PL9...32 B2
Belle Vue Rd PLYMST/WEM PL9...32 B2
Belle Vue Rd PLYMST/WEM PL9...32 C2
SALT PL12......8 D5
Bellevue Sq PLY PL1......23 F2
Bellingham Crs PLYMP PL7...21 F5
Belliver Wy PLYMP PL7......6 B2
Bellows Pk PLYMP PL8......35 F2
Bell Pk PLYMP PL7 *......21 E2
Belmont Pl EFF/MANN PL3...16 C5
Belmont St PLY PL1......2 E3
Belstone Cl PLYNW PL5......10 C3
Benbow St KEY/HAM/PCR PL2...16 B5
Bennets La SALT PL12......8 D3
Bennett St PLY PL1......24 A3
Beresford St
KEY/HAM/PCR PL2......16 B4
Berkshire Dr
KEY/HAM/PCR PL2......16 B4
Bernice Cl PLYE PL4......18 B5
Bernice Ter PLYE PL4......18 B5
Berrow Park Rd EFF/MANN PL3...17 C5
Berry Head Gdns PLYNE PL6...11 C5
Berry Pk SALT PL12......8 B2
Berry Park Cl
PLYMST/WEM PL9......33 E1
Berthon Rd PLYNE PL6......19 F2
Berwick Av PLYNW PL5......11 C3
Betjeman Wk PLYNW PL5......11 E3
Beverley Rd EFF/MANN PL3...18 B5
Beverston Wy PLYNE PL6......6 C5
Bewleys Pk SALT PL12......8 A4
Beyrout Pl PLY PL1......24 B1
Bickern Rd TOR PL11......23 F1
Bickham Park Rd
EFF/MANN PL3......17 F3
Bickham Rd PLYNW PL5......9 H4
Bickleigh Cl PLYNE PL6......12 A5
Bickleigh Down Rd PLYNE PL6...6 D3
Bicton Cl PLYNE PL6......12 D5
Biddick Dr KEY/HAM/PCR PL2...16 B3
Bideford Wk PLYNE PL6......19 E2
Bigbury Wk PLYNE PL6......19 E1
Biggin Hl PLYNE PL6......10 B2
Bilbury St PLYE PL4......3 J5
Billacombe Rd
PLYMST/WEM PL9......26 D4
Billacombe Vls
PLYMST/WEM PL9......27 F4
Billing Cl PLYNE PL6......18 B2
Billington Cl PLYNE PL6......18 B2
Bircham Vw PLYNE PL6......12 C5
Birch Cl PLYNE PL6......7 E4
The Birches PLYNE PL6......6 D5
Birchfield Av
KEY/HAM/PCR PL2......16 D3
Birch Pond Rd
KEY/HAM/PCR PL2......16 D3
Birchwood Gdns PLYMP PL7...21 E2
Birkbeck Cl PLYMP PL7......20 C2
Birkdale Cl SALT PL12 *......8 A4
Biscombe Gdns SALT PL12...9 E3
Bishops Pl PLY PL1......2 E6
Blackall Gdns SALT PL12......5 F5
Blackberry Cl
PLYMST/WEM PL9......26 D4
Blackeven Cl PLYNE PL6......6 D2
Blackeven Hl PLYNE PL6......6 D2
Blackfriars La PLY PL1......3 J5
Blackstone Crs PLYNE PL6......5 F5
Blackstone Cl
PLYMST/WEM PL9......33 H1
Blackthorn Cl PLYNE PL6......10 D3
Blairgowrie Rd PLYNW PL5...15 H1
Blake Gdns PLYNW PL5......11 E5
Blanchard Pl PLYMP PL7 *......20 C2
Blandford Rd EFF/MANN PL3...18 A4
Blaxton La PLYMP PL7......6 B5
Blenheim Rd PLYE PL4......3 J2
Blindwell Hl MBRK/KGSD PL10...30 C1
Bloomball Cl EFF/MANN PL3...18 B2
Bluebell Cl SALT PL12......8 B2
Blue Haze Cl PLYNE PL6......12 D1
Blunt's La PLYNE PL6......6 D5
Bodmin Rd PLYNW PL5......11 E4
Bond St PLYNE PL6......5 C5
Bonville Rd PLYNE PL6......5 F5
Boon's Pl PLY PL1......2 E2
Boringdon Av PLYNW PL5......15 H1
Boringdon Cl PLYMP PL7......20 B2
Boringdon Hl PLYMP PL7......20 C2
Boringdon Rd PLYMP PL7......20 B3
PLYMST/WEM PL9......26 A5
Borough Pk TOR PL11......14 C5
Borrowdale Cl PLYNE PL6......11 F1
Boscastle Gdns PLYNW PL5...11 E1
Boscawen Pl
PLYMST/WEM PL9......26 A5
Boscundle Rw SALT PL12 *......9 E4
Boswell Cl PLYNW PL5......10 D4

Boulden Cl PLYMP PL7......21 C4
Boulter Cl PLYMP PL7......6 C2
Bounds Pl PLY PL1......2 D1
The Bound MBRK/KGSD PL10...37 E1
Bourne Cl EFF/MANN PL3......18 D5
Boville La PLYMST/WEM PL9...28 A5
Bovisand Ct PLYMST/WEM PL9...38 A2
Bovisand La PLYMST/WEM PL9...38 A3
Bowden Park Rd PLYNE PL6...11 H5
Bowers Park Dr PLYNE PL6......7 E4
Bowers Rd KEY/HAM/PCR PL2...16 C5
Boxhill Cl PLYNW PL5......10 D3
Boxhill Gdns KEY/HAM/PCR PL2...17 E5
Bracken Cl PLYNE PL6......6 D4
Braddons Hl PLYMP PL7......19 H2
Bradfield Cl PLYNE PL6......13 E5
Bradford Cl PLYNE PL6......18 A2
Brake Rd PLYNW PL5......11 C4
Bramble Cl EFF/MANN PL3...18 B2
Bramfield Pl PLYNE PL6......18 B2
Bramley Rd EFF/MANN PL3...18 C5
Branker Rd KEY/HAM/PCR PL2...17 E3
Brandon Rd EFF/MANN PL3...18 C5
Brandreth Rd EFF/MANN PL3...17 H3
Branscombe Gdns PLYNW PL5...10 D3
Branson Cl PLYMP PL7......21 C4
Brayford Cl PLYNW PL5......10 D5
Breakwater Hl PLYE PL4......25 H4
Breakwater Rd
PLYMST/WEM PL9......26 C4
Brean Down Cl EFF/MANN PL3...18 A5
Brean Down Rd EFF/MANN PL3...17 C2
Brecon Cl EFF/MANN PL3......18 A2
Brentford Av PLYNW PL5......10 D3
Brentor Rd PLYE PL4......26 B2
Brest Rd PLYNE PL6......12 A3
Bretonside PLYE PL4......3 K4
Brianway SALT PL12......8 D5
Briardale Rd
KEY/HAM/PCR PL2......16 B3
Briarleigh Cl PLYNE PL6......13 F4
Briar Rd EFF/MANN PL3......17 H2
Brickfields Cl PLY PL1......24 B3
The Bridges SALT PL12......8 C5
Bridgwater Cl PLYNE PL6......12 B5
Bridle Cl PLYMP PL7......21 E2
Bridwell Cl PLYNW PL5......15 H1
Bridwell Rd PLYNW PL5......16 A1
Brimhill Cl PLYMP PL7......21 F5
Brixham Wk PLYNE PL6......19 E1
Broadland Gdns
PLYMST/WEM PL9......27 C4
Broadland La
PLYMST/WEM PL9......27 F4
Broadlands Cl PLYMP PL7......29 E1
Broadley Cl PLYNE PL6 *......6 B1
Broadley Park Rd PLYNE PL6...6 A2
Broad Park Rd PLYMST/WEM PL9...26 B5
Broad Park Rd EFF/MANN PL3...17 F3
Broad Wk SALT PL12......8 C5
Brockley Rd EFF/MANN PL3...18 C5
Brocks La MBRK/KGSD PL10...30 D2
Brockton Gdns PLYNE PL6......6 B5
Bromhead Ct PLYMP PL7......6 B4
Bromley Pl KEY/HAM/PCR PL2...16 C5
Bronte Pl PLYNW PL5......11 E3
Brook Cl PLYMP PL7......29 E1
Brookdown Ter SALT PL12......8 C5
Brookdown Vls SALT PL12......8 C5
Brookfield Cl PLYMP PL7......21 F4
Brooking Cl PLYNE PL6......12 A5
Brookingfield Cl PLYMP PL7...20 A4
Brooking Wy SALT PL12......8 A3
Brookside Cl PLYMST/WEM PL9...38 B4
The Brook SALT PL12......8 B5
Brookwood Rd
PLYMST/WEM PL9......28 B5
Broomfield Dr
PLYMST/WEM PL9......32 C1
Broom Pk SALT PL12......8 B4
Broom Pk PLYMST/WEM PL9...32 D2
Broughton Cl EFF/MANN PL3...17 H2
Brownhill La PLYMST/WEM PL9...38 A3
Browning Rd
KEY/HAM/PCR PL2......16 C4
Brownlow St PLY PL1......2 C5
Broxton Dr PLYMST/WEM PL9...27 E3
Brunel Av KEY/HAM/PCR PL2...16 B4
Brunel Vw SALT PL12 *......9 E3
Brunswick Pl
KEY/HAM/PCR PL2......16 B5
Brunswick Rd PLYE PL4......25 H3
Brynmoor Cl EFF/MANN PL3...18 A2
Brynmoor Pk EFF/MANN PL3...18 A3
Brynmoor Wk EFF/MANN PL3...18 A3
Buckfast Cl KEY/HAM/PCR PL2...16 B1
Buckingham Pl PLYNW PL5...10 A4
Buckland Cl PLYMP PL7......20 B2
Buckwell St PLY PL1......3 J4
Buddle Cl PLYMST/WEM PL9...33 F2
Budleigh Cl PLYMST/WEM PL9...33 F2
Budshead Rd PLYNW PL5......10 C2
PLYNW PL5......11 E2
Budshead Wy PLYNW PL5...11 C4
Buena Vista Cl PLYNE PL6......6 D5
Buena Vista Dr PLYNE PL6......6 C5
Buena Vista Gdns PLYNE PL6...6 C5
Buena Vista Wy PLYNE PL6...6 C5
Bulleid Cl KEY/HAM/PCR PL2...16 B1
Buller Cl PLYMP PL7......20 D5
Buller Pk SALT PL12......8 A3
Buller Rd TOR PL11......23 F1
Bulmer Rd PLYE PL4......26 A2
Bunyan Cl PLYNW PL5......11 E4
Burleigh La EFF/MANN PL3...17 E4
Burleigh Mnr EFF/MANN PL3...17 E4
Burleigh Park Rd
EFF/MANN PL3......17 F3
Burnard Cl PLYNE PL6......5 C4
Burnett Cl SALT PL12......8 B4
Burnett Rd PLYNE PL6......17 H1

Burnham Park Rd
EFF/MANN PL3......17 F2
Burniston Cl PLYMP PL7......29 E1
Burns Av PLYNW PL5......10 D4
Burrington Rd PLYNW PL5......10 C5
Burrington Wy PLYNW PL5...10 C5
Burrow Hl PLYMST/WEM PL9...33 E1
Burton Cl PLYNE PL6......6 B5
Burwell Cl PLYNE PL6......13 E5
Bush Pk PLYNE PL6......13 F3
Bute Rd PLYE PL4......18 A5
Butler Cl PLYNE PL6......6 B5
Butt Park Rd PLYNW PL5......11 E5
Byard Cl PLYNW PL5......10 A5
Byland Rd EFF/MANN PL3...18 A5
Byron Av PLYNW PL5......10 D4

C

Cabot Cl SALT PL12......8 C4
Cadover Cl PLYNE PL6......12 A5
Caernarvon Gdns
KEY/HAM/PCR PL2......16 D2
Calder Cl EFF/MANN PL3......18 C5
Caldicot Gdns PLYNE PL6......6 B5
Caledonia Cl PLYMP PL7......21 F4
California Gdns EFF/MANN PL3...18 D5
Callington Rd SALT PL12......8 B3
Calvez Cl MBRK/KGSD PL10...30 D1
Camber Rd PLYE PL4......2 C6
Camborne Cl PLYNW PL5......10 C1
Cambridge Rd
KEY/HAM/PCR PL2......16 B4
Camden St PLYE PL4......3 K2
Cameron Wy PLYNE PL6......12 B5
Camilla Ter KEY/HAM/PCR PL2...17 F2
Campbell Rd PLYMST/WEM PL9...27 F5
Camperdown St
KEY/HAM/PCR PL2......16 B5
Camperknowle Cl
MBRK/KGSD PL10......30 D1
Campian Cl SALT PL12......8 B2
Campion Cl PLYMP PL7......21 C4
Campion Vw PLYMST/WEM PL9...28 B5
Candish Dr PLYMST/WEM PL9...33 E2
Canefields Av PLYMP PL7......29 F1
Canhaye Cl PLYMP PL7......29 E1
Cann Gdns PLYNE PL6......5 F5
Cann St PLY PL1......23 H2
Cann Wood Vw PLYNE PL6......7 E4
Canterbury Dr PLYNW PL5......10 D2
Caradon Cl PLYNE PL6......12 A2
Caradon Ter SALT PL12......8 C2
Carbeile Rd TOR PL11......23 E1
Cardiff Cl PLYMP PL7......21 F5
Cardigan Rd PLYNE PL6......12 C5
Cardinal Av PLYNW PL5......16 A1
Careswell Av
KEY/HAM/PCR PL2......16 B1
Carew Av PLYNW PL5......10 D3
Carew Gdns PLYNW PL5......10 D3
SALT PL12......8 C5
Carew Gv PLYNW PL5......10 D3
Carew Ter TOR PL11......23 F2
Carey Ct SALT PL12......8 C5
Carisbrooke Rd PLYNE PL6......12 C5
Carlisle Rd PLYNE PL6......11 E5
Carlton Cl EFF/MANN PL3......18 B4
Carlton Ter PLYE PL4......25 H3
PLYNW PL5......16 A1
Carlyon Cl TOR PL11......14 D5
Carmarthen Rd PLYE PL4......26 B1
Carnock Rd KEY/HAM/PCR PL2...17 F2
Caroline Cl SALT PL12......8 A3
Caroline Pl PLY PL1......2 C5
Carpenter Rd
PLYMST/WEM PL9......27 F5
Carradale Rd PLYNE PL6......18 C2
Carroll Rd PLYNW PL5......11 E4
Carron La PLYNE PL6......6 D2
Castle Bank Gdns
EFF/MANN PL3......18 B4
Castle Carey Gdns
EFF/MANN PL3......18 B4
Castle Ct SALT PL12......8 C5
Castlehayes Gdns PLYMP PL7...20 C5
Castle Hl SALT PL12......14 A1
Castle La PLYMP PL7......20 C5
Castlemead Ct SALT PL12......8 B5
Castlemead Dr SALT PL12......8 B4
Castle Ri EFF/MANN PL3......18 B5
Castle St PLY PL1......3 J5
Castle Cl PLYE PL4......18 A5
Castle Vw SALT PL12......8 B5
Cathcart Av PLYE PL4......26 B2
Cathedral St PLY PL1......2 E3
Catherine St PLY PL1 *......3 H4
Cattedown Rd PLYE PL4......26 A4
Catterick Cl PLYNW PL5......10 A1
Cattewater Rd PLYE PL4......26 B5
Cavendish Rd PLYE PL4......26 B5
Cayley Wy PLYNW PL5......16 A1
Cecil Av PLYE PL4......26 A3
Cecil Cotts PLY PL1 *......2 D1
Cecil St PLY PL1......2 E1
Cedar Dr TOR PL11......22 C2
Cedarcroft Rd
KEY/HAM/PCR PL2......16 D2
Celandine Gdns PLYMP PL7...21 C4
Central Park Av PLYE PL4......25 E1
Central Rd PLY PL1......3 F6
Chaddiewood Av PLYMP PL7...29 F1
Chaddlewood Cl PLYMP PL7...29 E1
Chad Rd EFF/MANN PL3......18 C5
Chagford Wk PLYNE PL6......19 E1
Chalfield Cl PLYMST/WEM PL9...33 F2
Chalfield Ri PLYMST/WEM PL9...33 F2
Challock Cl PLYNE PL6......12 C2
Chamberlayne Dr PLYMP PL7...20 C3
Channel Park Av
EFF/MANN PL3......18 B4

Channel View Ter PLYNE PL4...26 A1
Channon Rd SALT PL12......8 A2
Chapeldown Rd TOR PL11......23 E2
Chapel St PLY PL1......24 A2
PLYE PL4......3 J2
Chapel Wy PLYNW PL1......18 A3
Chapmans Ope PLY PL1......23 H2
Chard Barton PLYNW PL5......10 D5
Chard Rd PLYNW PL5......10 A4
Charfield Dr PLYNE PL6......18 A1
Charles Cross PLY PL1......3 J3
Charles St PLY PL1......3 J2
Charles Ter EFF/MANN PL3...18 A3
Charlotte St KEY/HAM/PCR PL2...16 A5
Charlton Crs PLYNE PL6......12 A4
Charlton Rd PLYNE PL6......11 H5
Charnhill Cl PLYMST/WEM PL9...33 C1
Charnhill Wy PLYMST/WEM PL9...33 C1
Chatsworth Gdns PLYNE PL6...10 B5
Chaucer Wy PLYNE PL6......10 D5
Chedworth St PLYE PL4......3 K2
Chelmsford Pl PLYNW PL5...21 E4
Chelsea Gdns PLYNE PL6......11 E5
Chepstow Av PLYNE PL6......6 C5
Cheriton Cl PLYNW PL5......10 C5
Cherry Pk PLYMP PL7......29 E1
Cherry Tree Dr
PLYMST/WEM PL9......35 G2
Cherry Tree La PLYMP PL7......21 E5
Cheshire Dr PLYNE PL6......5 E5
Chesterfield Rd EFF/MANN PL3...18 B5
Chester Pl PLYE PL4......17 C5
Chestnut Av PLYMST/WEM PL9...32 C2
Chestnut Cl TOR PL11......22 D1
Chestnut Rd PLYE PL4......17 F2
Chichester Crs SALT PL12......8 C5
Childrey Gdns PLYNE PL6......12 C5
Childrey Wk PLYNE PL6......12 C5
Chilton Cl PLYNE PL6......18 B2
Chittleburn Hl
PLYMST/WEM PL9......34 C2
Chivenor Av PLYNE PL6......9 H2
Chubb Dr EFF/MANN PL3......16 D5
Chudleigh Rd PLYE PL4......18 A5
Church Cl PLYMP PL7......19 H2
Church Hl PLYNE PL6......12 B5
Church Hill Rd
PLYMST/WEM PL9......32 A1
Churchill Wk SALT PL12 *......8 B5
Churchill Wy EFF/MANN PL3...17 C5
Churchlands Cl PLYNE PL6......7 E4
Church Park Ct PLYNE PL6......7 E3
Church Park Rd PLYNE PL6......7 E3
Church Rd PLYMST/WEM PL9...27 C5
PLYMST/WEM PL9......39 C4
SALT PL12......8 B5
Church Row La PLYNW PL5......5 F5
Churchstow Wk PLYNE PL6...19 E1
Church St EFF/MANN PL3......16 C5
Churchtown V SALT PL12......8 B5
Church Wy PLYNW PL5......16 A1
Church Wy PLYNE PL6 *......5 F5
Citadel Rd PLY PL1......3 J5
Citadel Rd East PLY PL1......3 J5
Citadel Rd West PLY PL1......3 F5
Claremont St PLY PL1......3 F1
Clarence Cl PLY PL1......2 C3
Clarence Pl KEY/HAM/PCR PL2...16 A5
PLY PL1......2 C3
Clarence Rd TOR PL11......23 E1
Clare Pl PLYE PL4......25 H3
Clayton Pl PLYE PL4......26 B2
Clearbrook Av PLYNW PL5......10 A5
Clear Vw SALT PL12......8 C3
The Cleave MBRK/KGSD PL10...31 E5
Cleeve Gdns KEY/HAM/PCR PL2...16 C1
Clegg Av TOR PL11......22 C1
Clement Rd PLYMP PL7......21 F4
Clevedon Park Av
KEY/HAM/PCR PL2......16 D3
Cleveland Av PLYE PL4......26 A2
Clifford Cl PLYNW PL5......10 A4
Cliff Rd PLY PL1......3 F6
PLYMST/WEM PL9......39 C4
Clifton Av PLYMP PL7......20 C2
Clifton Cl PLYMP PL7......20 C2
Clifton Pl PLYE PL4......25 G1
Clifton St PLYE PL4......3 K1
Clinton Av PLYE PL4......26 A1
Clinton Ter MBRK/KGSD PL10...31 E5
Clittaford Rd PLYNE PL6......5 H4
The Close SALT PL12......8 A3
Clovelly Rd PLYE PL4......25 H4
Clovelly Wy PLYNE PL6......26 A5
Clover Ri PLYNE PL6......7 E5
Clowance Cl PLY PL1 *......24 B3
Clowance St PLY PL1......24 A3
Clyde St KEY/HAM/PCR PL2...16 B4
Coach House Ms
PLYMST/WEM PL9......33 H1
Cobbett Rd PLYNW PL5......10 D4
Cobb La PLYMST/WEM PL9...35 H1
Cobourg St PLY PL1......3 H2
Cockington Ct PLYNE PL6......13 E5
Cockington Wk PLYNE PL6...12 C5
Colborne Rd PLYNE PL6......12 A4
Coldrenick St PLYNW PL5......9 H5
Coldrenick St PLYMP PL7......20 B5
PLYNW PL5......9 H5
Coleman Dr PLYMST/WEM PL9...33 F3
Coleridge Av PLYNE PL6......11 H4
Coleridge Rd PLYE PL4......17 H5
Colesdown Hl
PLYMST/WEM PL9......27 C4
Colin Campbell Ct PLY PL1...3 F3
Collard Cl PLYMP PL7......29 E1
College Av PLYE PL4......17 C4
College Gv PLYE PL4......17 C5
College Rd KEY/HAM/PCR PL2...16 A4
College Vw EFF/MANN PL3...17 F5

Colliers Cl PLYMST/WEM PL9......39 H3
Collin Cl PLYNW PL5......9 H5
Collingwood Av PLYE PL4......26 A3
Collingwood Rd EFF/MANN PL3...24 C1
Collingwood Vls
EFF/MANN PL3......24 B1
Colne Gdns EFF/MANN PL3.....18 B4
Colston Cl PLYNE PL5......6 B5
Coltishall Cl PLYNW PL5......10 B2
Coltness Rd PLYMST/WEM PL9...33 H2
Coltsfield Cl PLYNW PL6......18 B4
Colwill Rd PLYNW PL6......13 E5
Colwyn Rd TOR PL11......23 E1
Combley Dr PLYNW PL6......12 D2
Commercial Ope PLYE PL4......25 H4
Commercial Rd EFF/MANN PL3...25 H5
Commercial St PLY PL4......25 H5
Compass Dr PLYMP PL7......21 E2
Compton Av EFF/MANN PL3......17 H4
Compton Knoll Cl
PLYMN PL3......18 A3
Compton Leigh
EFF/MANN PL3......18 A3
Compton Park Rd
EFF/MANN PL3......17 H4
Compton Vw EFF/MANN PL3.....18 A4
Congreve Gdns PLYNW PL5......11 E5
Coniston Gdns PLYNE PL6......11 H2
Connaught Av PLYE PL4......17 G5
Connaught La PLYE PL4......17 G5
Conqueror Dr PLYNW PL5......11 E5
Conrad Rd PLYNW PL5......11 E5
Consort Cl EFF/MANN PL3......17 G2
Constable Cl PLYNW PL5......11 H4
Constance Pl PLY PL1......2 C2
Constantine St PLYE PL4......3 J5
Convent Cl SALT PL12......8 C3
Conway Gdns
KEY/HAM/PCR PL2......16 D2
Conyngham Ct PLYNE PL6......18 A1
Cooban Ct PLYNE PL6......18 A1
Cookworthy Rd
KEY/HAM/PCR PL2......16 B3
Coombe La PLYNE PL6......5 E5
Coombe Pk MBRK/KGSD PL10..31 E5
SALT PL12......8 D4
Coombe Park Cl
MBRK/KGSD PL10......31 E5
Coombe Park La PLYNW PL5.....10 C3
Coombe Wy PLYNW PL5......10 D5
Copleston Rd PLYNE PL6......11 F1
Coppard Mdw PLYMP PL7......19 H5
Copper Beech Wy PLYNE PL6...6 C4
Coppers Pk PLYNE PL6......7 E4
Coppice Gdns PLYNW PL5......11 G4
Coppice Wood Dr PLYNE PL6...6 C4
Copse Cl PLYMP PL7......20 B5
Copse Rd PLYMP PL7......20 B5
Copthorne Gdns
PLYMST/WEM PL9......33 F2
Corea Ter PLY PL1......2 A7
Corfe Av EFF/MANN PL3......17 H2
Coringdean Cl PLYNE PL6......6 B5
Corner Brake PLYNE PL6......6 D4
Cornfield Gdns PLYMP PL7......21 F2
Cornwall Beach PLY PL1......2 D3
Cornwall St PLY PL1......2 F3
Cornwood Rd PLYMP PL7......21 F5
Cornworthy Cl
KEY/HAM/PCR PL2......16 C2
Coronation Pl PLYNW PL5......16 A1
Corondale Rd
KEY/HAM/PCR PL2......16 D2
Corporation Rd
KEY/HAM/PCR PL2......17 F2
Corsham Cl PLYNE PL6......6 B5
Cosdon Pl PLYNE PL6......11 H5
Cotehele Av KEY/HAM/PCR PL2..16 B4
PLYE PL4......26 A3
Cot Hl PLYMP PL7......19 H4
Cottage Ms PLYMP PL7......20 C5
Cotton Cl PLYMP PL7......20 D5
County Cl PLYMP PL7......21 E4
Courtenay St PLY PL1......3 G4
Courtfield Rd EFF/MANN PL3...17 H4
Courtland Crs PLYMP PL7......20 B2
Courtlands SALT PL12......8 C5
The Court PLYNE PL6......18 A1
Court Vw YLMP PL8......34 D5
Cove Meadow TOR PL11......15 E3
Coverdale Rd PLYNW PL5......10 D5
Cowdray Cl SALT PL12......8 C4
Cowdray Ter SALT PL12 *......8 C5
Cowley Rd PLYNW PL5......11 F4
Coypool Rd PLYMP PL7......19 G2
Crabtree Cl EFF/MANN PL3......19 F4
Crackston Cl PLYNE PL6......18 B2
Craigie Dr PLY PL1......2 C2
Craigmore Ter
KEY/HAM/PCR PL2......16 B4
Cramber Cl PLYNE PL6......6 C3
Cranbourne Av PLYE PL4......26 A1
Cranfield Cl PLYMP PL7......20 A2
Cranmere Rd EFF/MANN PL3...18 A3
Crantock Ter
KEY/HAM/PCR PL2......16 C4
Crashaw Cl PLYNW PL5......11 F3
Craven Av PLYE PL4......26 A1
Crawford Rd PLY PL1......2 A1
Crediton Wk PLYNE PL6......19 E1
Creedy Rd EFF/MANN PL3......18 C4
Cremyll Rd PLY PL11......23 F2
Cremyll St PLY PL1......2 B5
Crescent Av PLY PL1......3 F5
The Crescent PLY PL1......2 E5
YLMP PL8......35 E2
Cressbrook Cl PLYNE PL6......13 F4
Cressbrook Dr PLYNE PL6......13 F4
Cresthill Rd KEY/HAM/PCR PL2..16 D2
Croft Pk PLYNE PL6......6 C4
Cromarie Rd PLYE PL4......26 B5
Cromer Cl PLYNE PL6......6 A4
Cromwell Ga PLYNE PL6......6 C4
Cromwell Rd PLYE PL4......26 A3

Crookeder Cl PLYMST/WEM PL9..33 G2
Cross Hl KEY/HAM/PCR PL2......16 A5
Cross Pk YLMP PL8......35 F2
Cross Park Av PLYNE PL6......11 H5
Cross Park Rd
PLYNE PL6......11 H5
PLYNE PL6......11 H5
Crossway PLYMP PL7......20 B2
Crossway Av PLYNE PL6......11 H5
Crossways PLYMST/WEM PL9...39 G3
Crowndale Av EFF/MANN PL3...18 A3
Crownhill Rd PLYNW PL6......11 H4
Crownhill Fort Rd PLYNE PL6...11 H4
Crownhill Rd PLYNW PL6......10 C5
Crow Pk PLYE PL4......17 H4
Croydon Gdns PLYNW PL5......10 A2
Crozier Rd PLYE PL4......17 H5
Cuffe Rd EFF/MANN PL3......18 D3
Cuidrose Cl PLYNW PL5......10 A5
Culme Rd EFF/MANN PL3......18 A4
Culver Cl PLYNE PL6......18 A1
Culver Rd SALT PL12......8 D4
Culver Wy PLYNE PL6......18 A1
Culverwood Cl PLYMP PL7......21 G5
Cumberland Rd PLY PL1......2 A4
Cumberland St PLY PL1......2 A4
Cundy Cl PLYMP PL7......19 G2
Cunliffe Av PLYMST/WEM PL9...32 A1
Cunningham Rd PLYNW PL5......5 E3
Cunningham Wy SALT PL12 *....8 B5
Curlew Ms EFF/MANN PL3......18 C5
Curtis St PLY PL1......2 A3
Custom House La PLY PL1......2 C6
Cypress Cl PLYMP PL7......21 C4

D

Dale Av EFF/MANN PL3......18 C2
Dale Gdns PLYE PL4......25 F4
Dale Rd PLYE PL4......25 F4
Dalton Gdns PLYNW PL5......10 A3
Damerel Cl PLY PL1......24 B2
Danum Dr PLYMP PL7......29 F1
Darklake Cl PLYNE PL6......13 E1
Darklake La PLYNE PL6......6 D3
Darklake Vw PLYNE PL6......13 E1
Dark Street La PLYMP PL7......20 C4
Darmouth Wk PLYNE PL6......19 E1
Dart Cl EFF/MANN PL3......18 C5
Dartmeet Av EFF/MANN PL3.....18 C5
Dartmoor Vw PLYE PL4......18 B5
SALT PL12......8 C5
Darwin Crs EFF/MANN PL3......18 D4
Davenham Cl PLYNE PL6......6 B5
David Cl PLYMP PL7......20 D5
Davy Cl TOR PL11......22 D1
Davy Rd PLYNE PL6......12 C2
Dawes La MBRK/KGSD PL10....30 C2
Dawson Cl PLYNW PL5......10 A5
Daymond Rd PLYNW PL5......9 H4
Dayton Cl PLYNW PL5......11 G5
Deacon Cl SALT PL12......8 D5
Deacon Dr SALT PL12......8 D5
Dean Cross Rd
PLYMST/WEM PL9......27 E5
Dean Hl PLYMST/WEM PL9......27 E5
Dean Park Rd
PLYMST/WEM PL9......26 D5
Dean Rd PLYMP PL7......20 B2
Debden Cl PLYNW PL5......9 H2
Deeble Cl PLYMP PL7......20 C2
Deep La PLYMP PL7......20 A4
Deer Pk SALT PL12......8 D3
Deer Park Dr EFF/MANN PL3...18 C5
Defoe Cl PLYNW PL5......11 E4
Delacombe Cl PLYMP PL7......20 B5
De-la-Hay Av EFF/MANN PL3...24 D1
Delamere Rd PLYNE PL6......18 D2
The Dell PLYMP PL7......19 H3
Dengie Cl PLYNE PL6......21 F4
Denham Cl PLYNW PL5......11 G2
Dennis Cl PLYNW PL5......15 G2
Deptford Pl PLYE PL4......3 K1
Derby Rd PLYNW PL5......11 E2
Derriford Pk PLYNE PL6......12 A5
Derriford Rd PLYNE PL6......12 A3
Derry Av PLYE PL4......25 F1
Derrys Cross PLY PL1......3 F4
Derwent Av EFF/MANN PL3.....18 C4
Desborough La PLYE PL4......26 A2
Desborough Rd PLYE PL4......26 A2
Deveron Cl PLYMP PL7......21 E4
Devonia Cl PLYMP PL7......21 E4
Devonport Hl MBRK/KGSD PL10..31 E5
PLY PL1......24 B3
Devonport Rd
KEY/HAM/PCR PL2......16 C5
PLY PL1......24 C5
Devonshire St PLYE PL4......3 K2
Devon Ter PLY PL4......17 G5
Diamond Av PLYE PL4......25 H1
Dickens Rd PLYNW PL5......10 D4
Dickiemoor La PLYNW PL5......10 D3
Dieppe Cl PLY PL1......24 A2
Digby Gv PLYNW PL5......11 G4
Dingle Rd KEY/HAM/PCR PL2...16 C5
PLYMP PL7......20 A4
Dingwall Av PLYNW PL5......11 G3
Distine Cl EFF/MANN PL3......18 C2
Dittisham Wk PLYNE PL6......19 E1
Ditton Cl PLYNE PL6......18 A1
Dixon Pl KEY/HAM/PCR PL2......16 B5
Dockray Cl PLYNE PL6......18 A2
Dodbrook MBRK/KGSD PL10....30 C3
Doddridge Cl PLYMST/WEM PL9..33 F3
Dodges Farm Cl PLYNE PL6....13 E1
Dolphin Cl PLYMST/WEM PL9...33 F3
Dolphin Court Rd
PLYMST/WEM PL9......33 F3
Dolphin Sq PLYMST/WEM PL9...33 F1

Donkey La MBRK/KGSD PL10....30 A4
Donnington Dr EFF/MANN PL3...18 C2
Dorchester Av PLYNW PL5......11 F2
Doreena Rd PLYNW PL6......28 A5
Dormy Av EFF/MANN PL3......17 H4
Douglas Dr PLYMST/WEM PL9...33 G1
Douglass Rd EFF/MANN PL3....18 D3
Dovedale Rd KEY/HAM/PCR PL2..16 C2
Dove Gdns EFF/MANN PL3......18 D3
Dover Rd PLYNE PL6......13 E3
Dove Cl SALT PL12......8 A5
Downfield Dr PLYMP PL7......20 D4
Downgate Gdns
KEY/HAM/PCR PL2......17 F1
Downham Gdns PLYNW PL5......5 E4
Down Rd PLYMP PL7......21 G4
Downside Av PLYNE PL6......18 C2
Downton Cl PLYNE PL6......2 D2
Drake Circ PLY PL1......3 H2
Drake Cl PLYE PL4......25 H2
Drakefield Dr SALT PL12......9 E3
Drake Wy PLYMST/WEM PL9...27 E5
Drax Gdns PLYE PL6......17 G1
Drayton Rd PLYNW PL5......11 E5
The Drive EFF/MANN PL3......17 G2
Drummond Cl
KEY/HAM/PCR PL2......16 B2
Drummond Pl
KEY/HAM/PCR PL2......24 B1
Drunken Bridge Hl PLYMP PL7...28 A1
Dryburgh Crs
KEY/HAM/PCR PL2......16 C1
Dryden Av PLYNW PL5......11 E5
Ducane Wk PLYNE PL6......12 B5
Duckworth St
KEY/HAM/PCR PL2 *......16 C5
Dudley Gdns PLYNE PL6......18 B1
Dudley Rd PLYMP PL7......19 H4
Duke St PLY PL1......24 A3
Duloe Gdns KEY/HAM/PCR PL2..17 E1
Dumfries Av PLYNW PL5......11 F3
Dunclair Pk EFF/MANN PL3.....18 D4
Duncombe Av PLYNW PL5......10 B3
Dundonald St
KEY/HAM/PCR PL2......16 B5
Dunheved Rd SALT PL12......8 D4
Dunkeswell Cl
KEY/HAM/PCR PL2......16 B1
Dunley Wk PLYNE PL6......12 C5
Dunnet Rd PLYNE PL6......5 F5
Dunraven Dr PLYNE PL6......12 A1
Dunster Cl PLYMP PL7......21 G5
Dunstone Av PLYMST/WEM PL9..33 C1
Dunstone Cl PLYMST/WEM PL9...27 F5
Dunstone Dr PLYMST/WEM PL9..27 F5
Dunstone La PLYMST/WEM PL9..27 F5
Dunstone Rd EFF/MANN PL3....18 B5
PLYNW PL5......10 B5
Dunstone Vw
PLYMST/WEM PL9......27 G5
Durban Rd EFF/MANN PL3......17 F4
Durham Av PLYE PL4......26 A1
Durnford St PLY PL1......2 B5
Durrant Cl PLY PL1......2 B5
Durris Cl PLYNE PL6......12 D2
Durris Gdns PLYNE PL6......12 D2
Durwent Cl PLYMST/WEM PL9...32 A1
Duxford Cl PLYNW PL5......10 A2
Dynevor Cl EFF/MANN PL3......17 H2

E

Eagle Rd PLYMP PL7......21 G5
Earls Acre EFF/MANN PL3 *.....17 E5
The Earl's Dr MBRK/KGSD PL10..31 E5
Earls Mill Rd PLYMP PL7......20 C5
Earls Wood Cl PLYNE PL6......13 F3
Earls Wood Dr PLYNE PL6......13 F3
Eastbury Av PLYNW PL5......10 C4
Eastcote Cl PLYNE PL6......13 F3
East End PLYMST/WEM PL9 *...26 C4
Easterdown Cl
PLYMST/WEM PL9......27 F5
Eastern Wood Rd PLYMP PL7...21 H4
Eastfield Av PLYMST/WEM PL9...32 C1
Eastfield Crs EFF/MANN PL3....18 A3
East La MBRK/KGSD PL10......36 D3
East Park Av PLYE PL4......17 F5
East St PLY PL1......2 D4
Ebrington St PLYE PL4......3 J3
Eddystone Cl EFF/MANN PL3....18 D3
Eddystone Rd
PLYMST/WEM PL9......38 C1
Eddystone Ter PLY PL1......2 E7
Edgar Ter PLY PL1......18 A5
Edgcumbe Park Rd
EFF/MANN PL3......17 F3
Edgcumbe Rd SALT PL12......8 A1
Edgcumbe St PLY PL1 *......2 B4
Edinburgh St PLY PL1......24 A5
Edith Av PLYE PL4......26 A1
Edith St PLYNW PL5......9 H5
Edna Ter PLY PL4......17 F5
Edwards Cl PLYMP PL7......21 F5
Edwards Dr PLYMP PL7......21 F4
Effingham Crs EFF/MANN PL3...17 F2
Efford Crs EFF/MANN PL3......18 B3
Efford La EFF/MANN PL3......18 B3
Efford Pathway EFF/MANN PL3..18 C3
Efford Rd EFF/MANN PL3......18 B3
Efirst Av PLY PL1......24 B2
Egerton Crs PLYE PL4......26 A2
Egerton Pl PLYE PL4......26 A2
Egerton Rd PLYE PL4......25 H2
Eggbuckland Rd
EFF/MANN PL3......17 H3
Egret Cl MBRK/KGSD PL10......31 E1
Eight Acre Cl PLYMP PL7......21 G4
Elaine Cl PLYMP PL7......19 H4
Elburton Rd PLYMST/WEM PL9..27 G4
Eldad Hl PLY PL1......2 C2

Elder Cl PLYMP PL7......21 F4
Elford Crs PLYMP PL7......20 C2
Elford Dr PLYMST/WEM PL9.....26 C5
Elgin Crs PLYNW PL5......11 C4
Elim Ter KEY/HAM/PCR PL3......17 C4
Elliot St PLY PL1......16 A1
Elizabeth Pl PLYE PL4......3 J1
Elliot Sq TOR PL11......23 F1
Elliot St PLY PL1......3 G5
Elliott Cl SALT PL12......8 B4
Elliot Ter PLY PL1......3 G6
Elliot Terrace La PLY PL1......3 G6
Elliott Rd PLYE PL4......26 A3
Elliotts Hl YLMP PL8......35 E3
Elm Crs PLYE PL4......18 A5
Elmcroft KEY/HAM/PCR PL5....16 D2
Elm Cft PLYMP PL6 *......6 D5
Elm Gv PLYMP PL7......6 D5
Elm Rd PLYE PL4......17 H4
PLYMP PL7......6 D5
The Elms EFF/MANN PL3......24 C1
Elmwood Cl PLYNE PL6......12 C1
Elphinstone Rd
KEY/HAM/PCR PL2......17 E2
Elwell Rd SALT PL12......9 E4
Elwick Gdns EFF/MANN PL3.....18 B4
Embankment La
PLYMST/WEM PL9......26 B2
Embankment Road La North
PLYE PL4......25 H1
Emily Gdns PLYE PL4......25 H1
Emma Pl PLY PL1......2 B5
Emma Place Ope PLY PL1......2 B5
Endsleigh Park Rd
PLYE PL4......17 F5
Endsleigh Pl PLYE PL4......3 J1
Endsleigh Pl Ope PLYE PL4......3 J1
Endsleigh Rd PLYMST/WEM PL9..20 C2
Epping Crs PLYNE PL6......18 D2
Epworth Ter KEY/HAM/PCR PL2..16 B4
Eric Rd PLYE PL4......26 A2
Erith Av PLYMST/WEM PL9......32 A1
Erle Gdns PLYMP PL7......28 D1
Erlstoke Cl PLYNE PL6......12 D5
Erme Gdns PLYNE PL6......18 C4
Erme Plym Trail
PLYMST/WEM PL9......32 D1
PLYMST/WEM PL9......39 C3
Ermington Ter PLYE PL4......17 F5
Ernesettle Crs PLYNW PL5......9 H3
Ernesettle Grn PLYNW PL5......9 H2
Ernesettle La PLYNW PL5......5 G5
Esmonde Gdns PLYNW PL5......15 F1
The Esplanade PLY PL1......3 G6
Essa Rd SALT PL12......8 D4
Essex St PLY PL1......2 E2
Estover Cl PLYNE PL6......13 E2
Estover Rd PLYNE PL6......13 E2
Eton Av PLY PL1......3 G1
Eton Pl PLY PL1......3 G1
Eton St PLY PL1......3 G2
Eton Ter PLY PL1 *......3 G1
Evelyn Pl PLYE PL4......25 G1
Evelyn St PLYNW PL5......9 H5
Evenden Ct TOR PL11......23 E1
Exeter Cl PLYNE PL6......18 C2
Exeter St PLY PL1......3 J4
PLYE PL4......25 H2
Exmouth Rd PLY PL1......24 B1

F

Fairfax Ter KEY/HAM/PCR PL2...16 B5
Fairfield PLYMP PL7......20 B2
Fairfield Av KEY/HAM/PCR PL2...17 E2
Fairmead Ms SALT PL12......8 A4
Fairmead Rd SALT PL12......8 A3
Fairview Av EFF/MANN PL3......18 D4
Fairview Cl PLYNE PL6......19 E4
Fairway SALT PL12......8 A4
Fanshawe Wy
PLYMST/WEM PL9......32 C1
Faraday Rd PLYE PL4......26 B5
Farington Rd PLYE PL4......26 B1
Farm Cl PLYMP PL7......20 A3
Farm La PLYNW PL5......10 D4
SALT PL12......8 B5
Farnley Cl PLYNE PL6......6 B5
Fearnside Wy SALT PL12......8 A3
Federation Rd EFF/MANN PL3...18 C5
Regan Rd PLYNW PL5......9 H5
Fellows La PLY PL1......2 B2
Fellows Pl PLY PL1......2 B2
Fenten Pk SALT PL12......8 D5
Ferndale Av KEY/HAM/PCR PL2..16 A2
Ferndale Cl PLYNE PL6......16 D3
Ferndale Rd KEY/HAM/PCR PL2..16 A2
Fernleigh Rd PLYE PL4......17 H4
Ferrers Rd PLYNW PL5......10 A5
Ferry Rd EFF/MANN PL3......24 A5
Ferry Rd KEY/HAM/PCR PL2.....16 A4
Ferry St TOR PL11......23 F2
Feversham Pl PLYMP PL7......21 F5
Finch Cl PLYE PL4......18 C5
Findon Gdns PLYMST/WEM PL9..28 A5
Findon Gdns PLYNE PL6......12 D2
Finewell St PLY PL1......3 H4
Finnigan Rd PLYE PL4......26 B4
Fircroft Rd KEY/HAM/PCR PL2...16 D2
Firestone Cl PLYNE PL6......13 E1
Firs Cl PLYNE PL6......6 D4
PLYMST/WEM PL9......27 F4
Firtree Rd PLYMP PL6 *......7 E5
Fisgard Wy TOR PL11......22 D1
Fisher Rd EFF/MANN PL3......16 C4
Fistral Cl TOR PL11......14 D5
Fitzroy Rd PLY PL1......2 B1
Fitzroy Ter PLY PL1......2 A1
Flamborough Rd PLYNE PL6....10 A5
Flamsteed Crs PLYNW PL5......10 A5
Fleet St KEY/HAM/PCR PL2......16 A5

Fletcher Crs PLYMST/WEM PL9...3
Fletcher Wy PLYMST/WEM PL9...3
Fletemoor Rd PLYNW PL5......
Flora Cottages PLY PL1......
Flora Ct PLY PL1......
Flora St PLY PL1......
Florence Pl PLYE PL4......
Florence St PLYNW PL5......
Floyd Cl KEY/HAM/PCR PL2......
Foliot Av KEY/HAM/PCR PL2......
Foliot Rd KEY/HAM/PCR PL2......
Forder Hts PLYNE PL6......
Forder Hl MBRK/KGSD PL10......
Forder La MBRK/KGSD PL10......
Forder Valley Rd PLYNE PL6.....
Ford Park La PLYE PL4......
Ford Park Rd PLYE PL4......
Ford Rd PLYMST/WEM PL9......
Forest Av KEY/HAM/PCR PL2....
Foresters Rd PLYMST/WEM PL9..
Fore St MBRK/KGSD PL10......
PLY PL1......
PLYMP PL7......
PLYNW PL5......
SALT PL12......
TOR PL11......
Forest Vw PLYNE PL6......
Forge La SALT PL12......
Forresters Dr PLYNE PL6......
Fort Austin Av PLYNE PL6......
Fortescue Pl EFF/MANN PL3....
Forth Gdns PLYMP PL7......
Fort Ter PLYNE PL6......
The Fort MBRK/KGSD PL10......
Fosbrooke Ct EFF/MANN PL3...
Foulston Av PLYNW PL5......
Fountains Crs
KEY/HAM/PCR PL2......
Fox Field Cl EFF/MANN PL3......
Foxtor Cl PLYNW PL5......
Foxwood Gdns
PLYMST/WEM PL9......
PLYNW PL5......
Foyle Cl PLYMP PL7......
Francis St PLY PL1......
Frankfort Ga PLY PL1......
Franklyns' PLYE PL6......
Franklyns Cl PLYNE PL6......
Fraser Pl PLYNW PL5......
Fraser Rd PLYNW PL5......
Frederick St East PLY PL1......
Frederick St West PLY PL1 *.....
Fredington Gv
Freedom Sq PLYE PL4......
Freemans Whf PLY PL1......
Fremantle Gdns
KEY/HAM/PCR PL2......
Fremantle Pl
KEY/HAM/PCR PL2......
Frensham Av PLYNE PL6......
Frensham Gdns PLYNE PL6......
Frewin Gdns PLYNE PL6......
Friars' La PLY PL1......
Friary St PLYE PL4......
Frith Rd SALT PL12......
Frobisher Ap PLYNW PL5......
Frobisher Dr SALT PL12......
Frobisher Wy TOR PL11......
Frogmore Av PLYNE PL6......
Frogmore Ct PLYNE PL6......
Frome Cl PLYMP PL7......
Frontfield Crs PLYNE PL6......
Fullerton Rd KEY/HAM/PCR PL2..
Furland Cl PLYMST/WEM PL9....
Furneaux Av
KEY/HAM/PCR PL2......
Furneaux Rd
KEY/HAM/PCR PL2......
Fursdon Cl PLYMST/WEM PL9...
Furse Pk PLYNW PL5......
Furzeacre Cl PLYMP PL7......
Furzehatt Av
Furzehatt Park Rd
Furzehatt Rd PLYMST/WEM PL9..
Furzehatt Wy
Furzehill Rd PLYE PL4......
PLYMST/WEM PL9......

G

Gabber La PLYMST/WEM PL9....
Galileo Cl PLYMP PL7......
Galsworthy Cl PLYNW PL5......
Galva Rd PLYMP PL7......
Ganges Rd KEY/HAM/PCR PL2..
Ganna Park Rd EFF/MANN PL3..
Gara Cl PLYMST/WEM PL9......
Garden Cl PLYMP PL7......
Garden Crs PLY PL1......
Garden Park Cl
Garden St KEY/HAM/PCR PL2...
Gards La PLYNW PL5......
Garfield Ter EFF/MANN PL3......
Garrett St MBRK/KGSD PL10....
Garrick Cl PLYNW PL5......
Garrison Cl PLY PL1......
Garston Cl PLYMST/WEM PL9...
Gascoyne Ter
PLYMP PL7 *......
Gashouse La PLYE PL4......
Gasking St PLY PL4......
Gdynia Wy PLYE PL4......
Geasons La PLYMP PL7......

...ge Av PLYMP PL7 20 C3
...ge Pk PLYMP PL7 20 D4
...ge Pl PLY PL1 2 C4
...ge Sq PLY PL1 24 B5
...on La PL4 3 J2
...rd Pl EFF/MANN PL3 17 F5
...ed Terrace Rd EFF/MANN PL3 17 F4
...rt Ct PLYMP PL7 21 F3
...rt La KEY/HAM/PCR PL2 13 B5
...on Rd MBRK/KGSD PL3 18 B4
...on Rd SALT PL12 8 A2
...avon Rd EFF/MANN PL3 17 C4
...ourn Cl EFF/MANN PL3 17 C2
...lower Rd EFF/MANN PL3 17 F4
...eagle Av EFF/MANN PL3 17 H3
...eagle Rd EFF/MANN PL3 17 H3
...field Cl PLYNE PL6 6 D5
...field La PLYNE PL6 12 D1
...field Wy PLYNE PL6 7 E5
...holt Cl PLYNE PL6 6 D5
...holt Rd PLYNE PL6 6 C5
...more Av KEY/HAM/PCR PL2 16 B4
...naven Cl PLYMP PL7 21 C3
...Park Av PLYE PL4 25 F1
...Rd PLYE PL4 17 H4
...side Ri PLYMP PL7 10 C1
...cor Rd EFF/MANN PL3 17 C2
...wood Rd EFF/MANN PL3 17 C3
...cester Ct PLY PL1 * 21 F3
...cester Pl PLY PL1 3 J1
...A? TOR PL11 22 C1
...Cl TOR PL11 22 D1
...ling Gdns PLYNE PL6 5 C4
...en Sq PLYMP PL7 * 20 C3
...smith Gdns PLYNW PL5 11 F3
...leve Cl PLYMST/WEM PL5 33 E2
...win Av PLYNE PL6 6 A5
...win Crs KEY/HAM/PCR PL2 16 B4
...eford La TOR PL11 22 A3
...ewell Hi PLYNE PL6 18 C1
...ewell Park Rd YMST/WEM PL9 33 F1
...ewell Rd YMST/WEM PL9 33 F1
...ewell Ter MST/WEM PL9 33 F1
...on Ct SALT PL12 * 8 B4
...on Ter PLYE PL4 25 F1
...vela Cl PLYMST/WEM PL9 11 C4
...vela Gdns MST/WEM PL9 33 F2
...d Ridge Rd YMST/WEM PL9 32 D1
...ton Rd PLYE PL4 17 C5
...tley Gdns PLYNE PL6 11 H5
...by Ct PLY PL1 24 A2
...by Cn PLY PL1 24 A2
...by Wy PLY PL1 24 A2
...d Hotel Rd PLY PL1 3 F6
...d Pde PLY PL1 2 E2
...ge Rd PLYMP PL7 20 D5
...ttham Cl PLYMP PL7 19 H5
...tley Gdns EFF/MANN PL3 18 A5
...ence Cl PLYNE PL6 11 C1
...sendale Av YMST/WEM PL9 16 B2
...umere Wy SALT PL12 8 B2
...esend TOR PL11 23 F1
...esend Gdns TOR PL11 23 F1
...esend Wk PLYNW PL5 9 H2
...Crs PLYNW PL5 15 C1
...e Berry Rd PLYNE PL6 11 C5
...t Churchway YMST/WEM PL9 27 C5
...tfield Rd EFF/MANN PL3 18 B2
...clands Crs Y/HAM/PCR PL2 16 C3
...clands Pl Y/HAM/PCR PL2 16 C4
...t Orchard Cl
...t Western Rd PLY PL1 2 E6
...e Woodford Dr PLYMP PL7 19 H5
...e Cl PLYMP PL7 20 D4
...acres PLYMST/WEM PL9 27 F4
...nbank Av PLYE PL4 25 H1
...nbank Rd PLYE PL4 25 H1
...nbank Ter PLYE PL4 25 H1
...YMP PL7 * 20 C3
...ndale Rd Y/HAM/PCR PL2 16 C2
...nfield Rd SALT PL12 8 B4
...nfinch Crs SALT PL12 8 A3
...nhill Cl PLYMST/WEM PL9 33 F2
...nland MBRK/KGSD PL10 30 D2
...nlees Dr PLYMP PL7 29 F1
...n Pk MBRK/KGSD PL10 * 31 E5
...n Park Rd
...Green MBRK/KGSD PL10 31 E5
...ALT PL12 * 8 A4
...nway Av PLYMP PL7 19 H5
...nwood Pk Cl PLYMP PL7 21 F3
...nwood Park Rd YMP PL7 21 F5
...fell Av SALT PL12 8 A3
...fell Gdns SALT PL12 * 8 A3
...ville Ct PLYE PL4 21 C4
...ville Rd PLYE PL4 26 A2

Grenville Road La South PLYMST/WEM PL9 26 B2
Gresham Ct PLYNW PL5 5 E4
Greystoke Av PLYNE PL6 18 C2
Griffin Wy PLYMST/WEM PL9 34 A1
Griggs Cl PLYMP PL7 21 F5
Grimspound Cl PLYNE PL6 19 E1
Grizedale Rd PLYNE PL6 18 D2
Grosvenor Rd PLYNE PL6 11 H4
Grove Pk TOR PL11 22 C1
The Grove EFF/MANN PL3 16 C5
PLYMST/WEM PL9 26 D4
Guildford Cl PLYNW PL5 11 C3
Guildford St PLYE PL4 3 K2
Guildhall Sq PLY PL1 2 D4
Gurnard Wk EFF/MANN PL3 18 C5
Gurney Cl TOR PL11 22 D1
Guy Miler Wy PLYNW PL5 10 D5
Guys Quay PLY PL4 3 K4
Gwithian Cl TOR PL11 14 D5
Gwyn Rd PLYE PL4 26 A1
Gwyn Road Ter PLYE PL4 26 A2

H

Haddington Rd KEY/HAM/PCR PL2 16 A5
Halcyon Rd KEY/HAM/PCR PL2 16 C3
Hallerton Cl PLYNE PL6 13 E5
Hailey Gdns PLYNW PL5 10 A5
Hamble Cl EFF/MANN PL3 18 D2
Ham Cl KEY/HAM/PCR PL2 16 D2
Ham Dr KEY/HAM/PCR PL2 16 D1
Ham Gn KEY/HAM/PCR PL2 16 D1
Ham Green La KEY/HAM/PCR PL2 16 C2
Hamilton Gdns PLYE PL4 17 F5
Hamoaze Av PLYNW PL5 15 H1
Hamoaze Pl PLY PL1 23 H2
Hamoaze Rd TOR PL11 23 F2
Hampton St PLYE PL4 3 J5
Hancock Cl PLYNE PL6 6 D5
Hanover Rd EFF/MANN PL3 18 B4
Harbour Av PLYE PL4 3 K4
PLYNW PL5 16 A1
Harbour Vw SALT PL12 8 A2
Hardings Cl SALT PL12 8 A2
Hardy Crs PLYNW PL5 17 C1
Harebell Cl SALT PL12 8 A2
Harewood Cl PLYMP PL7 20 C4
Harewood Crs PLYNW PL5 10 B2
Hargood Ter KEY/HAM/PCR PL2 16 B5
Hargreaves Cl PLYNW PL5 10 B4
Harlech Cl EFF/MANN PL3 18 A2
Haroldsleigh Av PLYNW PL5 11 C4
Hartland Cl PLYNE PL6 6 A4
Hartley Av EFF/MANN PL3 17 H5
Hartley Park Gdns EFF/MANN PL3 17 H5
Hartley Rd EFF/MANN PL3 17 C3
Hartwell Av PLYMST/WEM PL9 28 B5
Harvey St TOR PL11 23 F1
Harwell Ct PLY PL1 2 C4
Harwell St PLY PL1 2 C4
Harwood Av PLYNW PL5 3 E4
Haseston Cl PLYMP PL7 29 F1
Hastings St PLY PL1 2 C4
Hastings Ter PLY PL1 3 F2
Haswell Cl PLYNE PL6 18 A1
Hat La MBRK/KGSD PL10 30 D5
Hatshill Cl PLYNE PL6 13 C3
Hatshill Farm Cl PLYNE PL6 7 C2
Havelock Ter KEY/HAM/PCR PL2 24 B1
Haweswater Cl PLYNE PL6 11 C2
Hawkers Av PLYE PL4 3 J4
Hawkinge Gdns PLYNW PL5 10 A2
Hawkins Cl PLYNE PL6 12 A1
Hawks Pk SALT PL12 8 A4
Hawthorn Av TOR PL11 22 D1
Hawthorn Cl PLYMST/WEM PL9 32 C2
PLYNE PL6 6 D4
Hawthorn Dr PLYMST/WEM PL9 39 C4
Hawthorn Park Rd PLYMST/WEM PL9 39 C4
Hawthorns SALT PL12 8 A4
Hawthorn Wy EFF/MANN PL3 18 B2
Haxter Cl PLYNE PL6 6 B2
Haydon Gv PLYNW PL5 9 C5
Haye Rd PLYMST/WEM PL9 27 H3
Haye Rd South PLYMST/WEM PL9 28 A5
Hayes Rd PLYMST/WEM PL9 26 C5
Haystone Wy PLY PL1 2 E1
Hayston Pl PLYNW PL5 10 B5
Haytor Cl PLYNW PL5 10 B3
Hazel Cl PLYNE PL6 6 D5
Hazel Dr PLYMST/WEM PL9 28 A5
Hazel Gv PLYMST/WEM PL9 28 A5
Hazelwood Crs PLYMST/WEM PL9 28 B5
Hazelwood Dr PLYNE PL6 6 D3
Headland Pk PLYE PL4 3 C1
Hedgerow Cl PLYMP PL7 21 F5
Hedingham Cl PLYMP PL7 21 C5
Hedingham Gdns PLYNE PL6 6 A4
Hele Cl PLYNE PL6 7 E2
Hele Gdns PLYMP PL7 20 D5
Hele's Ter PLYE PL4 26 B3
Hemerdon Hts PLYMP PL7 21 E5
Hemerdon La PLYMP PL7 21 C1
Hemerdon Wy PLYMP PL7 20 B5
Henderson Pl KEY/HAM/PCR PL2 16 B3
Hendwell Cl PLYNE PL6 5 C5

Henley Dr PLYNW PL5 5 E4
Herbert Pl KEY/HAM/PCR PL2 16 A5
Herbert St KEY/HAM/PCR PL2 16 A5
Hereford Rd PLYNW PL5 10 D1
Heritage Cl SALT PL12 8 A3
Hermitage Rd EFF/MANN PL3 17 C4
Heron Cl MBRK/KGSD PL10 30 D1
Herschel Gdns PLYNW PL5 10 A5
Hertland Wk KEY/HAM/PCR PL2 16 C2
Hessary Dr PLYNE PL6 6 C2
Hessary Vw SALT PL12 8 C5
Hetling Cl PLY PL1 2 E2
Hewer's Rw PLYE PL4 3 K3
Hewitt Cl SALT PL12 8 C3
Hexham Pl KEY/HAM/PCR PL2 16 C1
Hexton Hill Rd PLYMST/WEM PL9 32 B1
Heybrook Av PLYNW PL5 9 H5
Heybrook Dr PLYMST/WEM PL9 38 B5
Hickory Dr PLYMP PL7 21 F4
Hick's La PLYE PL4 3 J4
Highbury Crs PLYMP PL7 20 B2
Highclere Gdns PLYNE PL6 6 B3
Higher Anderton Rd MBRK/KGSD PL10 30 D2
Higher Churchway PLYMST/WEM PL9 27 C5
Higher Compton Rd EFF/MANN PL3 17 H5
Higher Efford Rd EFF/MANN PL3 18 B4
Higher Mowles EFF/MANN PL3 18 B5
Higher Park Cl PLYMP PL7 29 F1
Higher Port Vw SALT PL12 8 A2
Higher Rw MBRK/KGSD PL10 * 31 E5
Higher Stert Ter PLYE PL4 26 A2
Higher Woodford La PLYMP PL7 20 A2
Highfield Cl EFF/MANN PL3 18 C4
Highfield Dr PLYMST/WEM PL9 39 C3
Highglen Dr PLYMP PL7 21 F5
High Rd PLYMST/WEM PL9 39 F5
High St EFF/MANN PL3 2 B4
Hill Cl PLYMP PL7 20 B5
Hill Crest EFF/MANN PL3 18 B5
Hillcrest Cl PLYMP PL7 21 E4
Hillcrest Dr PLYMP PL7 21 E5
Hilldale Rd PLYMST/WEM PL9 33 E1
Hilldean Cl PLYNW PL5 5 H4
Hill La EFF/MANN PL3 17 H2
Hill Park Crs PLYE PL4 25 C1
Hillsborough PLYE PL4 17 H5
Hillsdune Rd EFF/MANN PL3 17 C3
Hillside Av PLYE PL4 8 D5
SALT PL12 8 D5
Hillside Crs PLYMST/WEM PL9 27 F4
Hillside Rd SALT PL12 8 C5
Hill St PLYE PL4 3 K3
Hill Top Crest PLYNW PL5 10 A4
Hilton Av PLYNW PL5 11 E5
Hingston Ct PLYNE PL6 18 A1
Himandale Rd PLYNW PL5 10 B3
HM Dockyard PLY PL1 23 H1
Hobart St PLY PL1 2 D4
Hobbs Crs SALT PL12 8 A3
Hodge Cl PLY PL12 8 A3
Hoe Ap PLY PL1 3 H5
Hoe Gdns PLY PL1 3 H5
Hoegate St PLY PL1 3 J5
Hoe Rd PLY PL1 3 H5
Hoe St PLY PL1 3 H5
Hogarth Cl PLYMST/WEM PL9 33 H1
Holborn Pl PLYMP PL7 * 20 C5
Holborn St PLYE PL4 25 H3
Holcombe Dr PLYMST/WEM PL9 33 F2
Holcroft Cl SALT PL12 8 B4
Holdsworth St EFF/MANN PL3 25 E1
Holebay Cl PLYMST/WEM PL9 33 C2
Hollacombe Brake PLYMST/WEM PL9 39 H1
Holland Rd EFF/MANN PL3 17 C3
PLYMP PL7 21 H4
PLYMST/WEM PL9 33 F1
Holloway Gdns PLYMST/WEM PL9 33 C2
Hollowgutter La TOR PL11 22 A2
The Hollows PLYMST/WEM PL9 27 H4
Holly Ct PLYNE PL6 19 E2
Hollycroft Rd PLYMST/WEM PL9 18 A2
Holly Park Cl PLYNW PL5 10 C1
Holly Park Dr PLYNW PL5 10 C1
Hollywood Ter PLY PL1 2 D2
Holman Ct KEY/HAM/PCR PL2 17 E1
Holmans Buildings PLY PL1 23 H2
Holmbush Wy YLMP PL8 35 E5
Holmer Down PLYNE PL6 6 D4
Holmes Av EFF/MANN PL3 18 B4
Holmwood Av PLYMST/WEM PL9 33 E2
Holme Cha PLYNE PL6 6 B4
Holtwood Rd PLYNE PL6 6 D4
Holwell Cl PLYMST/WEM PL9 33 C2
Holyrood Pl PLY PL1 3 C6
Home Farm Rd PLYMST/WEM PL9 27 E4
Home Pk KEY/HAM/PCR PL2 16 B5
Home Park Av EFF/MANN PL3 17 H4
Home Park Rd SALT PL12 9 E3
Homer Pk SALT PL12 9 C2
Homer Park La South PLYMST/WEM PL9 32 C2
Homer Ri PLYMST/WEM PL9 27 H5
Home Sweet Home Ter PLYE PL4 26 A3
Honcray PLYMST/WEM PL9 32 D2
Honeysuckle Cl PLYNE PL6 7 E4
SALT PL12 8 A2
Honicknowle Gn PLYNW PL5 10 D3
Honicknowle La PLYNW PL5 10 D5
Hooe Hl PLYMST/WEM PL9 32 C2
Hooe La PLYMST/WEM PL9 32 D4

Hooe Rd PLYMST/WEM PL9 32 C2
Hooksbury Av PLYMP PL7 29 F1
Hopton Cl PLYNE PL6 17 H1
Hornbrook Gdns PLYNE PL6 5 F5
Hornby St KEY/HAM/PCR PL2 16 A5
Hornchurch La PLYNW PL5 10 A2
Hornchurch Rd PLYNW PL5 10 A2
Horn Cross Rd PLYMST/WEM PL9 27 E5
Horn La PLYMST/WEM PL9 27 E5
YLMP PL8 35 E2
Horsham La PLYNW PL5 4 D4
PLYNW PL5 11 E4
Horswell Cl PLYMP PL7 21 H4
Hosford Cl PLYMST/WEM PL9 33 F5
Hospital Rd PLYE PL4 3 K1
Hotham Pl PLY PL1 2 C1
Houldsworth Rd KEY/HAM/PCR PL2 16 C5
Houndiscombe Rd PLYE PL4 3 C1
Hounster Dr MBRK/KGSD PL10 30 B2
Hounster Hl MBRK/KGSD PL10 30 B3
Housman Cl PLYNW PL5 11 F3
Howard Cl PLYNW PL5 11 F3
SALT PL12 8 A1
Howard Rd PLYMST/WEM PL9 27 E4
How St PLYE PL4 3 J4
Humber Cl EFF/MANN PL3 18 D3
Hungerford Rd KEY/HAM/PCR PL2 16 C5
Hunter Cl PLYNE PL6 11 H4
Huntingdon Gdns PLYNW PL5 11 F2
Huntley Pl EFF/MANN PL3 18 C5
Hurland Rd PLYNE PL6 13 E4
Hurrabrook Gdns PLYNE PL6 13 E5
Hurrell Cl PLYNE PL6 5 F5
Hurst Cl PLYMST/WEM PL9 33 F2
Hutchings Cl PLYNE PL6 5 F5
Huxham Ct PLYNE PL6 18 A1
Huxley Cl PLYMP PL7 20 D2
Hyde Park Rd EFF/MANN PL3 17 C4

I

Ilbert St PLY PL1 3 F1
Ince Cl TOR PL11 14 D5
Inchkeith Rd PLYNE PL6 5 F5
Ingra Brt EFF/MANN PL3 18 A5
Ingra Wk PLYNE PL6 18 A1
Innsworke Cl MBRK/KGSD PL10 31 E1
Innsworke Crs MBRK/KGSD PL10 31 E1
Inverdene EFF/MANN PL3 17 F4
Ipswich Cl PLYNW PL5 11 C2
Ivanhoe Rd PLYNW PL5 9 H4
Ivydale Rd PLYE PL4 17 H5

J

Jackman's Meadow MBRK/KGSD PL10 31 E4
Jackson Cl PLYNW PL5 16 B1
Jackson Pl KEY/HAM/PCR PL2 16 B5
Jago Av TOR PL11 23 E1
James Cl PLYMST/WEM PL9 27 H5
James Pl PLY PL1 3 H1
James St PLY PL1 24 A3
PLYE PL4 3 H2
Jasmine Gdns PLYMP PL7 21 F4
PLYE PL4 7 E5
Jean Crs EFF/MANN PL3 18 B3
Jedburgh Crs KEY/HAM/PCR PL2 16 C1
Jeffery Cl PLYNE PL6 5 F5
Jellicoe Rd PLYNW PL5 11 C5
Jenkins Cl PLYMST/WEM PL9 33 C2
Jennycliff La PLYMST/WEM PL9 32 A2
Jennys Combe Cl PLYMST/WEM PL9 33 F3
Jephson Rd PLYE PL4 26 B1
Jinkin Av PLYE PL4 25 H1
John La PLYE PL4 3 H1
John St KEY/HAM/PCR PL2 24 A1
Jubilee Ct SALT PL12 * 8 A4
Jubilee Rd PLYNW PL5 10 B3
Jubilee Ter PLYE PL4 26 B2
Julian St PLYE PL4 26 A3
Julian Wk PLYNE PL6 7 E5
Jump Cl PLYNE PL6 6 C2
Juniper Wy PLYMP PL7 21 F4

K

Kathleaven St PLYNW PL5 9 H5
Kay Cl PLYMP PL7 20 D2
Keat St KEY/HAM/PCR PL2 16 A5
Kedlestone Av PLYNW PL5 10 C4
The Keep SALT PL12 8 A4
Kelly Cl PLYMST/WEM PL9 15 C2
Kelvin Av PLYE PL4 26 A1
Kempe Cl KEY/HAM/PCR PL2 16 B3
Kempton Ter TOR PL11 23 F1
Kendal Pl PLYNW PL5 11 C2
Kenilworth Rd KEY/HAM/PCR PL2 16 D2
Kenley Gdns PLYNW PL5 10 B2
Kenmare Dr PLYMP PL7 21 H4
Kenn Cl PLYNW PL5 10 D3
Kennel Hl PLYMP PL7 20 B5
Kennel Hill Cl PLYMP PL7 20 A5
Kennet Cl EFF/MANN PL3 18 B4
Kensington Rd PLYE PL4 17 H5
Kent Rd KEY/HAM/PCR PL2 16 B4
Keppel Pl KEY/HAM/PCR PL2 16 B5
Keppel St KEY/HAM/PCR PL2 16 B5
Keppel Ter KEY/HAM/PCR PL2 * 16 B5
Kernow Cl TOR PL11 22 C1

Ker St Ope PLY PL1 * 24 A2
Ker St PLY PL1 24 A3
Kestrel Cl PLYNE PL6 6 D3
Kestrel Pk PLYNW PL5 * 10 D5
Keswick Crs PLYNE PL6 6 C2
Keyes Cl PLY PL1 24 B2
Keyham Rd KEY/HAM/PCR PL2 16 A5
Keyham St PLYNW PL5 16 A1
Khyber Cl TOR PL11 23 E1
Kidwelly Cl PLYMP PL7 21 H5
Kiel Pl EFF/MANN PL3 18 D4
Killigrew Av SALT PL12 8 B5
Kiln Cl MBRK/KGSD PL10 37 E1
PLYNW PL5 15 C1
Kimberly Dr PLYNE PL6 6 D5
King Edward Rd SALT PL12 8 D4
Kingfisher Cl PLYNE PL6 7 E5
Kingfisher Wy PLYMST/WEM PL9 26 C5
Kings Cl PLYNE PL6 * 7 E5
Kings Ct PLY PL1 2 A1
Kingsland Gardens Cl EFF/MANN PL3 17 C5
Kingsley Av TOR PL11 23 F2
Kingsmill Rd SALT PL12 8 B1
King's Rd PLY PL1 2 A3
PLYNW PL5 10 B5
King's Tamerton Rd PLYNW PL5 10 A5
Kingston Cl PLYMP PL7 21 E4
Kingston Dr PLYMP PL7 21 E5
King St MBRK/KGSD PL10 30 C2
PLY PL1 2 C3
TOR PL11 23 E1
Kingsway MBRK/KGSD PL10 31 F5
Kingsway Gdns PLYNE PL6 11 H3
Kingswear Crs PLYNE PL6 12 B5
Kingswood Park Av EFF/MANN PL3 17 F5
Kinnaird Crs PLYNE PL6 5 C4
Kinross Av PLYE PL4 26 A1
Kinsale Rd PLYNW PL5 10 B3
Kinterbury Rd PLYNW PL5 15 F1
Kinterbury St PLY PL1 3 J4
Kinterbury Ter PLYNW PL5 15 F1
Kinver Cl PLYNE PL6 12 D2
Kipling Gdns PLYNW PL5 11 F4
Kirkby Pl PLY PL4 3 H1
Kirkdale Gdns KEY/HAM/PCR PL2 16 D2
Kirkland Cl PLYNE PL6 6 C4
Kirkstall Cl KEY/HAM/PCR PL2 16 B1
Kirkwall Rd PLYNW PL5 11 C3
Kirton Pl EFF/MANN PL3 18 B4
Kit Hill Crs PLYNW PL5 15 C1
Kitley Vw YLMP PL8 35 F2
Kitley Wy PLYNW PL5 9 H5
Kitter Dr PLYMST/WEM PL9 33 F2
Knapps Cl PLYMST/WEM PL9 34 A1
Kneele Gdns PLYNE PL6 12 C1
Knighton Rd PLYE PL4 25 H2
PLYNE PL6 13 F5
Knill Cross MBRK/KGSD PL10 30 C2
The Knoll PLYNE PL6 19 H5
Knowland Cl PLY PL1 24 B1
Knowle Av KEY/HAM/PCR PL2 16 A3
Kynance Cl TOR PL11 14 D5

L

Laburnum Dr PLYMST/WEM PL9 39 C3
Laburnum Gv PLYNE PL6 * 13 E1
Ladysmith Rd PLYE PL4 26 A1
Ladywell Pl PLYE PL4 3 K2
Laira Av EFF/MANN PL3 18 D5
Laira Br PLYMST/WEM PL9 26 C3
Laira Bridge Rd PLYMST/WEM PL9 26 C3
Laira Park Crs PLYE PL4 18 B5
Laira Park Pl PLYE PL4 18 B5
Laira Park Rd PLYE PL4 18 B5
Laira Pl PLYE PL4 26 A2
Laira St PLYE PL4 26 A2
Lake Ms MBRK/KGSD PL10 * 30 C2
Lake Rd PLYMST/WEM PL9 32 B1
Lakeside Dr PLYNW PL5 10 A1
Lake View Cl PLYNW PL5 4 D5
Lakeview Dr PLYNW PL5 10 C1
Lalebrick Rd PLYMST/WEM PL9 32 B2
Lambert Rd PLYNW PL5 4 D5
Lambhay Hi PLY PL1 3 J6
Lambhay St PLY PL1 3 J6
Lamerton Cl PLYMP PL7 10 D3
Lamorna Pk TOR PL11 14 C5
Lancaster Gdns PLYNW PL5 11 F2
Lander Rd SALT PL12 8 D5
Landrake Cl PLYNW PL5 15 C1
Lands Pk PLYMST/WEM PL9 27 F5
The Lane PLYMP PL7 20 B5
Langage Cl PLYNE PL6 12 D5
Langdale Gdns PLYNE PL6 12 D5
Langdon Ct PLYMST/WEM PL9 33 H1
Langdon Down Wy TOR PL11 22 C1
Langerwell Cl SALT PL12 8 A3
Langerwell La SALT PL12 8 A3
Lang Gv PLYMST/WEM PL9 27 H5
Langham Pl PLYE PL4 26 A2
Langhill Rld EFF/MANN PL3 17 F4
Langley Cl PLYNE PL6 6 A4
Langley Crs PLYNE PL6 5 H4
Langmead Rd PLYNE PL6 18 C1
Langmore Cl PLYNE PL6 18 A1
Langstone Rd KEY/HAM/PCR PL2 17 E2
Lanhydrock Rd PLYE PL4 25 H2
Lansdowne Rd PLYNE PL6 11 H4
Larch Cl SALT PL12 8 A3
Larch Dr PLYNE PL6 7 E4
Larkham Cl PLYMP PL7 20 A3
Larkham La PLYMP PL7 20 A3
Lark Hl KEY/HAM/PCR PL2 16 C3

Latham CI PLYNE PL8......18 A2
Latimer CI PLYMP PL7......21 F4
Launceston CI PLYNE PL6......6 B4
Laura Dene KEY/HAM/PCR PL2......16 C2
Laurel Dr PLYNE PL6......13 E1
Laurel Rd KEY/HAM/PCR PL2......16 C2
Lavington CI PLYMP PL7......21 F4
Lavinia Dr PLYMP PL7......21 G4
Lawn CI PLYMP PL7......21 G4
The Lawns PLYNW PL5......11 G5
    TOR PL11......15 E5
Lawson Gv PLYMST/WEM PL9......26 D5
Leander Wy PLYNW PL5......11 F4
Leanway SALT PL12......8 B4
Leatfield Dr PLYNE PL6......11 H2
Leatherby CI PLYNE PL6......5 G4
Leat Wk PLYNE PL6......6 C2
Legis Wk PLYNE PL6......6 C3
Leigham Manor Dr PLYNE PL6......19 F1
Leigham St PLY PL1......5 F4
Leigh Ct PLYNE PL6......18 A1
Leigh La PLYNE PL6......6 D1
Leighton Rd EFF/MANN PL3......17 C1
Lentney CI PLYMST/WEM PL9......38 B5
Lester CI EFF/MANN PL3......18 B3
Lewes Gdns PLYNE PL6......11 E2
Leyford CI PLYMST/WEM PL9......39 H5
Leypark Dr PLYNE PL6......12 D4
Leypark Wk PLYNE PL6......13 E4
Liddle Wy PLYMP PL7......21 H5
Lifton Rd PLYE PL4......26 A5
Lilac CI PLYMST/WEM PL9......32 C2
Limerick PI PLYE PL4......26 A2
The Limes PLYNE PL6......11 F4
Lincoln Av PLYE PL4......17 F2
Lincoln Av PLYE PL4......26 A1
Linden Ter PLYE PL4......26 A2
Linkadells PLYMP PL7......20 B3
Linketty La East PLYNE PL6......20 A4
Linketty La East PLYNE PL6......12 A5
Linketty La West
    EFF/MANN PL3......17 G2
Linnet Ct SALT PL12......8 A4
Linton CI PLYNW PL5......5 E3
Linton Rd PLYNW PL5......5 E3
Lippell Dr PLYMST/WEM PL9......32 D1
Lipson Av PLYE PL4......26 A1
Lipson Rd PLYE PL4......3 K3
Lipson V PLYE PL4......18 A5
Lipstone Crs PLYE PL4......26 A1
Liscawn Ter TOR PL11......23 F1
Liskeard Rd SALT PL12......8 A3
Lisson Gv PLYE PL4......17 G5
Lister CI PLYMP PL7......20 D5
Litchaton Crs PLYMP PL7......19 H2
Litchaton Wy PLYMP PL7......19 H2
Litchfield CI PLYMP PL7......21 F3
Little Ash Gdns PLYNW PL5......9 F5
Little Ash Rd PLYNW PL5......9 F5
Little Dock La PLYNW PL5......10 C4
Little Down La PLYNE PL6......7 E1
Little Fancy CI PLYNE PL6......6 C4
Little La MBRK/KGSD PL10......31 E5
    PLYMST/WEM PL9......32 D4
Little Point Crs
    MBRK/KGSD PL10......30 D2
Littleton PI KEY/HAM/PCR PL2......16 B5
Littlewood CI PLYMP PL7......21 E5
Lizard CI PLYNE PL6......5 H4
Lockington Av PLYMP PL7......20 B3
Locks Wk PLY PL1......24 A3
Lockyer Ct PLY PL1 *......3 G5
Lockyer Rd EFF/MANN PL3......17 G4
Lockyers Quay PLY PL4......25 H3
Lockyer St PLY PL1......3 G5
Lockyer Ter SALT PL12 *......9 F4
Lodge La PLYMST/WEM PL9......34 D2
Lofoten CI PLY PL1......24 A2
Loftus Gdns PLYNW PL5......9 G4
Lollabury Rd SALT PL12......8 C3
Lonbrook Av PLYMP PL7......20 B3
Longbrook St PLYMP PL7......20 B3
Longbridge CI PLYNE PL6......19 F3
Longbridge Rd PLYE PL4......18 C5
    PLYNE PL6......19 F2
Longbrook Barton PLYMP PL7......20 B4
Longcause PLYMP PL7......20 D5
Long Close Ter PLYMP PL7......21 C4
Long Down Gdns PLYNE PL6......13 E3
Longfield PI PLYMST/WEM PL9......25 H1
Longfield Vls PLYMST/WEM PL9......26 D4
Longlands Dr
    PLYMST/WEM PL9......38 B3
Long Ley EFF/MANN PL3......18 B3
Long Meadow PLYMP PL7......20 B2
Longmeadow CI PLYMP PL7......20 B2
Longmeadow Rd SALT PL12......8 C1
Long Park CI
    PLYMST/WEM PL9......33 F2
Long Park Dr PLYMP PL7......6 D4
Long Park Rd SALT PL12......8 B4
Long Rowden EFF/MANN PL3......17 G3
Longstone Av PLYNE PL6......6 A5
Longview Rd SALT PL12......8 C1
Longview Ter EFF/MANN PL3......18 B3
Longwood CI PLYMP PL7......21 E5
Looe St PLY PL4......3 J4
Looseleigh CI PLYNE PL6......12 A2
Looseleigh La PLYNE PL6......11 G1
Looseleigh Pk PLYNE PL6......11 G1
Lopes Dr PLYNE PL6......6 C2
Lopes Rd KEY/HAM/PCR PL2......16 B5
Lopwell CI PLYNE PL6......11 H1
Lorrimore Av
    KEY/HAM/PCR PL2......16 B4
Lotherton CI PLYMP PL7......29 F1
Loughboro Rd PLYNE PL6......6 B4
Louert Rd EFF/MANN PL3......17 H3
Lower Anderton Rd
    MBRK/KGSD PL10......30 D2
Lower Compton Rd
    EFF/MANN PL3......17 H4
Lower Farm Rd PLYMP PL7......21 H4
Lower Fore St SALT PL12......9 E4

Lower Park Dr
    PLYNW PL9......33 F3
Lower Port Vw SALT PL12......8 D4
Lower Ridings PLYMP PL7......21 F2
Lower Saltram
    PLYMST/WEM PL9......26 C5
Lowerside KEY/HAM/PCR PL2......16 B1
Lower St PLYE PL4......3 K4
Lower Rd PLYMST/WEM PL9......39 F3
Lucas La PLYMP PL7......20 B3
Lucas Ter PLYE PL4......26 B2
Ludlow Rd EFF/MANN PL3......17 G3
Lulworth Dr PLYNE PL6......6 B4
Lundy CI PLYNE PL6......5 H4
Luxmore CI PLYNE PL6......13 E5
Lych CI PLYMST/WEM PL9......32 B1
Lydcot Wk PLYNE PL6......6 C3
Lydford Park Rd
    PLYE PL4......17 F4
Lydia Wy PLYE PL4......25 H1
Lympne Av PLYNW PL5......10 B1
Lyndhurst CI
    KEY/HAM/PCR PL2......17 E3
Lyndhurst Rd
    EFF/MANN PL3......17 E3
Lyndrick Rd EFF/MANN PL3......17 G2
Lynher Ct SALT PL12 *......8 D5
Lynher Dr SALT PL12......8 C5
Lynher St PLYNW PL5......9 H4
Lynmouth CI PLYMP PL7......20 A2
Lynwood Av PLYMP PL7......19 G3

M

Macadam Rd PLYE PL4......26 A4
Macaulay Crs PLYNW PL5......10 B1
Macey St TOR PL11......23 F1
Mackenzie PI PLYNW PL5......9 G5
Madden Rd PLY PL1......24 A2
Maddock CI PLYMP PL7......29 E1
Maddock Dr PLYMP PL7......21 E5
Madeira Rd PLY PL1......3 K6
Magdalen Gdns PLYMP PL7......28 D1
Magnolia CI PLYMP PL7......21 F4
Maida Vale Ter PLYE PL4......17 H5
Maidenwell Rd PLYMP PL7......21 F4
Maidstone PI PLYNW PL5......10 A2
Maine Gdns KEY/HAM/PCR PL2......16 B2
Mainstone Av PLYE PL4......26 A3
Maitland Dr EFF/MANN PL3......17 H1
Maker La MBRK/KGSD PL10......30 D5
Maker Rd TOR PL11......23 E2
Maker Vw EFF/MANN PL3......24 D1
Mallard CI PLYMP PL7......20 B2
Malmesbury CI
    KEY/HAM/PCR PL2......16 D1
Malory CI PLYNW PL5......11 F4
Manadon CI PLYNW PL5......11 G5
Manadon Dr PLYNW PL5......11 G5
Manby Gdns PLYNW PL5......10 B2
Manifold Gdns PLYE PL4......18 B5
Mannamead Av
    EFF/MANN PL3......17 H4
Mannamead Rd
    EFF/MANN PL3......17 G2
Manor Bourne Rd
    PLYMST/WEM PL9......38 C2
Manor Gdns PLY PL1......2 D4
Manor La EFF/MANN PL3......18 D4
Manor Pk SALT PL12 *......8 B4
Manor Park CI PLYMP PL7......20 D5
Manor Park Dr PLYMP PL7......20 D5
Manor St PLY PL1......2 D3
Manston CI PLYMST/WEM PL9......27 E4
Mantle Gdns PLYNW PL5......15 H1
Maple Av TOR PL11......23 E1
Maple CI PLYNE PL6......7 E5
Maple Gv PLYE PL4......17 F5
    PLYMP PL7......19 H4
Maple Wy PLYNE PL6......12 D2
Mardon CI PLYNW PL5......10 B1
Margaret Pk EFF/MANN PL3......17 C1
Marina Rd PLYNE PL6......10 B3
Marina Ter PLYE PL4......18 A5
Marine Dr PLYMST/WEM PL9......38 B4
Maristow Av
    KEY/HAM/PCR PL2......16 B2
Maristow CI PLYNW PL5......11 G1
Market Av PLY PL1......3 F5
Market CI PLY PL1 *......2 B4
Market Rd PLYMP PL7......20 B4
Market St MBRK/KGSD PL10......37 E1
    PLY PL1......2 B5
Market Wy PLY PL1 *......3 G5
Marlborough CI SALT PL12......8 D5
Marlborough Rd PLYE PL4......3 J1
Marlborough Rw PLY PL1......24 A2
Marlborough St PLY PL1......24 A2
Maridon CI PLYNW PL5......10 D3
Marlow Gdns
    PLYMST/WEM PL9......33 F2
Marrowbone Slip PLYE PL4......25 H3
Marryat Gdns PLYNW PL5......11 G5
Marshall Rd PLYMP PL7......19 G4
Marsh CI PLYMST/WEM PL9......27 F5
Marsh Mills EFF/MANN PL3......19 F5
Marsh Mills Pk PLYNE PL6......19 F5
Martin La PLY PL1 *......2 E4
    PLYE PL4......3 K4
Martin St PLY PL1......2 D5
Martlesham PI PLYNW PL5......10 B2
Marvland Gdns
    KEY/HAM/PCR PL2......16 B2
Mary Seacole Rd PLY PL1......2 C3
Masefield Gdns PLYNW PL5......10 D5
Masterman Rd
    KEY/HAM/PCR PL2......16 B5

Maunsell CI KEY/HAM/PCR PL2......16 B2
Maxwell Rd PLYE PL4......26 B4
Maybank Rd PLYE PL4......26 A2
Maybrook Dr SALT PL12......8 B4
Mayers Wy PLYMST/WEM PL9......32 D1
Mayfair Crs PLYE PL6......12 B5
Mayflower CI
    PLYMST/WEM PL9......27 F5
Mayflower Dr
    KEY/HAM/PCR PL2......16 D4
Mayflower St East PLY PL1......3 G2
Mayflower St West PLY PL1......3 G2
Maynarde CI PLYMP PL7......21 F4
May Ter PLYE PL4......25 H2
Meadfoot Ter PLYE PL4......17 H4
Meadow La PLYMP PL7......21 H5
Meadow Dr SALT PL12......8 B2
    YLMP PL8......34 D5
Meadowfield PI PLYMP PL7......29 F1
Meadowlands PLYNE PL6......6 D4
Meadow Pk PLYMST/WEM PL9......32 C2
Meadow Ri PLYMP PL7......21 H5
Meadowside PLYMST/WEM PL9......27 F5
The Meadows TOR PL11......14 C5
Meadowsweet Pk SALT PL12......8 A4
Meadow View Rd PLYMP PL7......20 A4
Meadow Wy PLYMP PL7......20 B2
The Mead PLYMP PL7......20 A2
Meadway SALT PL12......8 B5
Meavy Av PLYNW PL5......11 G4
Meavy Wy PLYNW PL5......11 G4
Medland Crs PLYNE PL6......5 F5
Medway PI EFF/MANN PL3......18 D5
Melbourne St PLY PL1......2 E1
Melrose Av KEY/HAM/PCR PL2......16 D1
Melville Rd KEY/HAM/PCR PL2......16 D1
Mena Park Rd
    PLYMST/WEM PL9......27 H5
Meraefield CI PLYMP PL7......19 H4
Meraefield Dr PLYMP PL7......20 A5
Meraefield Ri PLYMP PL7......20 A5
Meraefield Rd PLYMP PL7......19 H5
    PLYMST/WEM PL9......27 H2
Meredith Rd KEY/HAM/PCR PL2......17 E2
Merlin CI PLYNE PL6......6 D3
Merrivale Rd
    KEY/HAM/PCR PL2......16 C2
    PLYNW PL5......10 D3
Mersey CI EFF/MANN PL3......18 D2
The Mews EFF/MANN PL3......24 B1
    PLY PL1......2 D4
Mewstone Av
    PLYMST/WEM PL9......39 H3
Michael Rd EFF/MANN PL3......18 A4
Mid Churchway
    PLYMST/WEM PL9......27 G5
Middle Down CI
    PLYMST/WEM PL9......33 G2
Middlefield Rd PLYNE PL6......5 H5
Middle Rd PLYMST/WEM PL9......39 F4
Middleton Wk PLYNW PL5......9 H2
Milch Pk SALT PL12 *......8 A3
Mildmay St PLYE PL4......3 K1
Milehouse Rd EFF/MANN PL3......16 C5
Miles Mitchell Av PLYNE PL6......12 A5
Milford La PLYNW PL5......10 C2
Military Rd EFF/MANN PL3......18 C2
Millbay Rd PLY PL1......2 C5
Mill Br PLY PL1......2 C2
Miller Ct PLY PL1......2 C5
Miller Wy PLYNE PL6......12 D3
Millhouse Pk TOR PL11......23 E2
Mill La TOR PL11......23 E2
Millpool Head
    MBRK/KGSD PL10......30 C2
Millpool Rd MBRK/KGSD PL10......30 D1
Mill Rd MBRK/KGSD PL10......30 D1
Mills Rd PLY PL1......24 B2
Mill View Gdns
    MBRK/KGSD PL10 *......30 D2
Mill View Rd MBRK/KGSD PL10......30 D1
Millway PI PLYMST/WEM PL9......38 A5
Millwood Dr PLYNE PL6......13 E5
Milne PI KEY/HAM/PCR PL2......24 B1
Milton CI PLYNW PL5......11 E4
Milton Ct PLYE PL4......26 A3
Minerva CI PLYMP PL7......21 E5
Minses CI PLYMST/WEM PL9......28 A5
Mirador PI PLYE PL4......26 A1
Mitchell CI PLYMST/WEM PL9......32 D2
Modbury Ct PLYNW PL5......10 D5
Molesworth Rd EFF/MANN PL3......24 C1
    PLY PL1......2 C1
    PLYMP PL7......19 H3
Molesworth Ter
    MBRK/KGSD PL10......30 D2
Mollison Rd PLYNW PL5......10 A4
Molyneaux CI
    KEY/HAM/PCR PL2......24 B1
Monica Wk PLYE PL4......25 H1
Monmouth Gdns PLYNW PL5......11 E2
Montacute Av PLYNW PL5......10 C4
Montgomery CI SALT PL12......8 B3
Montpelier Rd
    KEY/HAM/PCR PL2......17 E2
Monument St PLY PL1......24 A3
Moon La PLYE PL4......3 K5
Moon St PLYE PL4......3 K3
Moorcroft CI
    PLYMST/WEM PL9......27 G5
Moorfield Av EFF/MANN PL3......18 C2
Moorland Av EFF/MANN PL3......18 C2
Moorland Dr PLYMP PL7......20 C5
Moorland Gdns PLYMP PL7......20 D5
Moorland Rd PLYMP PL7......20 C4
Moorlands La SALT PL12......8 A1
Moorland Vw
    PLYMST/WEM PL9......27 H5
    PLYNE PL6......12 A1
    SALT PL12......8 D3
Moor La PLYNW PL5......10 A5
Moor Vw KEY/HAM/PCR PL2......16 B4
    TOR PL11......23 F1

Moor View Ter PLYE PL4......17 G5
Moreton Av PLYNE PL6......11 H5
Morice St PLY PL1......24 A2
Morice Sq PLY PL1......24 A2
Morlaix Dr PLYNE PL6......12 A2
Morley La PLYMP PL7......19 G4
Morley Ct PLY PL1......3 F3
Morley View Rd PLYMP PL7......20 A3
Morrish Pk PLYMST/WEM PL9......33 F1
Morshead Rd PLYNE PL6......11 G4
Mortain Rd SALT PL12......8 B4
Mortimore CI SALT PL12......8 B4
Morwell Gdns
    KEY/HAM/PCR PL2......16 C3
Moses CI PLYNE PL6......5 G4
Mostyn Av PLYE PL4......18 A5
Mote Pk SALT PL12......8 A5
Mothecombe Wk PLYNE PL6......13 E5
Moulton CI PLYMP PL7......21 F5
Mountbatten CI
    PLYMST/WEM PL9......32 D1
Mountbatten Wy
    PLYMST/WEM PL9......32 D1
Mount Gould Av PLYE PL4......26 B1
Mount Gould Crs PLYE PL4......26 B1
Mount Gould Rd PLYE PL4......26 A1
Mount Pleasant
    MBRK/KGSD PL10......30 C2
Mount Stone Rd PLY PL1......2 B7
Mount St PLY PL1......24 A3
    PLYE PL4......3 K2
Mount Tamar CI PLYNW PL5......10 A4
Mowhay Rd KEY/HAM/PCR PL2......16 A4
Mudge Wy PLYMP PL7......20 C4
Mulberry CI PLYNE PL6......7 E4
Mulberry Rd SALT PL12......8 C4
Mulgrave St PLY PL1......3 G5
Mullet Av EFF/MANN PL3......18 C5
Mullet CI EFF/MANN PL3......18 C5
Mullet Rd EFF/MANN PL3......18 C5
Mullion CI TOR PL11......14 D5
Murdock Rd TOR PL11......22 D1
Mutley Pln PLYE PL4......17 G5
Mutley Plain La PLYE PL4......17 G5
Mutley Rd EFF/MANN PL3......17 C4
Mylor CI KEY/HAM/PCR PL2......17 F1
Myrtles Ct SALT PL12......8 B2
Myrtleville KEY/HAM/PCR PL2......16 C1

N

Nancarrows SALT PL12......8 A4
Napier St PLY PL1......24 B1
Napier Ter PLYE PL4......17 G5
Nash CI PLYMP PL7......21 E4
Neal CI PLYMP PL7......29 F1
Neath Rd PLYE PL4......26 A1
Nelson Av PLY PL1......24 B1
Nelson St PLYE PL4......3 K1
Nelson Ter PLYNE PL6......18 D1
Nepean St KEY/HAM/PCR PL2......16 B5
Neswick St PLY PL1......2 D5
Nettlehayes PLYMST/WEM PL9......28 B5
Netton CI PLYMST/WEM PL9......33 H1
Nevada CI EFF/MANN PL3......18 D5
New Barn HI PLYMP PL7......28 C1
Newbury CI PLYNW PL5......10 D2
Newcastle Gdns PLYNW PL5......10 D2
New George St PLY PL1......3 H3
Newman Rd PLYNW PL5
    SALT PL12......8 D3
Newnham CI PLYMP PL7......21 E2
Newnham Rd PLYMP PL7......20 D2
Newnham Wy PLYMP PL7......20 D3
New Park Rd PLYMP PL7......21 E5
New Passage HI PLY PL1......24 A1
Newport St MBRK/KGSD PL10......30 C2
    PLY PL1......24 A3
New Rd MBRK/KGSD PL10......37 E1
    PLYNE PL6......6 D1
    SALT PL12......8 D5
New Road CI MBRK/KGSD PL10......31 E5
New St MBRK/KGSD PL10......30 C2
Newton Av PLYNW PL5......10 A4
Newton Gdns PLYNW PL5......10 A4
New Wood CI PLYNE PL6......7 E3
Nicholson Rd PLYNW PL5......11 C4
Nightingale CI
    PLYMST/WEM PL9......28 A5
Nilch Pk SALT PL12......8 A5
Norfolk CI EFF/MANN PL3......18 C5
Norfolk Rd EFF/MANN PL3......18 C5
Normandy HI PLYNW PL5......9 F4
Normandy Wy PLYNW PL5......9 G4
Normanton CI PLYNW PL5......10 D1
North Cross PLY PL1......3 G1
North Down Crs
    KEY/HAM/PCR PL2......24 B1
North Down Gdns
    KEY/HAM/PCR PL2......16 B5
North Down Rd
    KEY/HAM/PCR PL2......16 B5
Northesk St KEY/HAM/PCR PL2......16 C5
North HI PLYE PL4......3 J2
Northoff Av PLYNW PL5......9 H2
North Park Vls SALT PL12......9 F4
North Prospect Rd
    KEY/HAM/PCR PL2......16 C2
North Rd SALT PL12......8 D5
    TOR PL11......23 F2
North Rd East PLYE PL4......3 H1
North Rd West PLY PL1......2 D2
Northumberland St
    PLYNW PL5......16 A1
Northumberland Ter PLY PL1......3 H5
North Weald Gdns PLYNW PL5......10 A1
Norton Av PLYE PL4......26 A1
Norwich Av PLYNW PL5......10 C1
Notre Dame CI PLYNE PL6......11 H1
Notte St PLY PL1......3 C5
Novorossisk Rd PLYNE PL6......13 G4

Nursery CI PLYNW PL5......

O

Oakapple CI PLYMP PL7......
Oak Apple CI SALT PL12......
Oakcroft Rd KEY/HAM/PCR PL2......
Oakdene Ri KEY/HAM/PCR PL2......
Oak Dr PLYNE PL6......
Oakfield CI PLYMP PL7......
Oakfield PI PLYE PL4......
Oakfield Rd PLYMP PL7......
Oakfield Terrace Rd PLYE PL4......
Oakham Rd PLYNW PL5......
Oaklands CI PLYNE PL6......
Oaklands Dr SALT PL12......
Oaklands Gn SALT PL12......
Oak Tree CI PLYNE PL6......
Oak Tree Pk PLYNE PL6......
Oakwood CI PLYNE PL6......
Oates Rd KEY/HAM/PCR PL2......
Ocean St KEY/HAM/PCR PL2......
Octagon St PLY PL1......
Okehampton CI PLYMP PL7......
Old Chapel Wy
    MBRK/KGSD PL10......
Old Farm Rd PLYNW PL5......
Old Ferry Rd SALT PL12......
Old George St PLY PL1......
Old Laira Rd EFF/MANN PL3......
Oldlands CI PLYNE PL6......
The Old Laundry PLY PL1......
Old Mill Ct PLYMP PL7......
Old Park Rd EFF/MANN PL3......
Old Plymouth Rd
    EFF/MANN PL3......
Old Priory PLYMP PL7......
Old Rd YLMP PL8......
Old School Rd PLYNW PL5......
Old Town St PLY PL1......
Old Warleigh La PLYNW PL5......
The Old Whf PLYMST/WEM PL9......
Old Woodlands Rd PLYNW PL5......
Onslow Rd KEY/HAM/PCR PL2......
Orchard Av PLYNE PL6......
Orchard CI PLYMP PL7......
    PLYMST/WEM PL9......
Orchard La PLYMP PL7......
Orchard Rd KEY/HAM/PCR PL2......
Orchardton Ter
    PLYMST/WEM PL9......
Ordnance St PLY PL1......
Oregon Wy EFF/MANN PL3......
Oreston Rd PLYMST/WEM PL9......
Osborne PI PLY PL1......
Osborne St KEY/HAM/PCR PL2......
Osprey Gdns PLYMST/WEM PL9......
Outland Rd KEY/HAM/PCR PL2......
Overdale Rd KEY/HAM/PCR PL2......
Overton Gdns EFF/MANN PL3......
Oxford Av PLYNW PL5......
Oxford Gdns EFF/MANN PL3......
Oxford PI PLY PL1......
Oxford St PLY PL1......
Oxford Ter PLY PL1 *......

P

Packington St
    KEY/HAM/PCR PL2......
Paddock CI PLYMST/WEM PL9......
    SALT PL12......
Palace St PLY PL1......
Palmerston St PLY PL1......
Parade PLY PL1......
Parade Rd PLYNW PL5......
The Parade MBRK/KGSD PL10 *......
Paradise PI PLY PL1......
Paradise Rd PLY PL1......
Park Av PLY PL1......
    PLYMST/WEM PL9......
Park CI PLYMP PL7......
Park Crs PLYMST/WEM PL9......
Parker CI PLYMP PL7......
Parker Rd KEY/HAM/PCR PL2......
Parkesway SALT PL12......
Parkfield Dr PLYNE PL6......
Park La PLYMST/WEM PL9......
Park Place La EFF/MANN PL3......
Park Rd EFF/MANN PL3......
    TOR PL11......
Parkway Ct PLYNE PL6 *......
The Parkway PLYNE PL6......
Parkwood CI PLYNE PL6......
Parnell CI PLYNE PL6......
Parr La PLYE PL4......
Parr St PLYE PL4......
Parsons CI PLYMST/WEM PL9......
Pasley St KEY/HAM/PCR PL2......
Pasley St East
    KEY/HAM/PCR PL2......
Patna PI PLY PL1......
Paton Watson Quadrate
    PLY PL1......
Pattendale CI EFF/MANN PL3......
Pattinson CI PLYNE PL6......
Pattinson Dr PLYNE PL6......
Peacock Av TOR PL11......
Peacock CI PLYNE PL6......
Pearn Gdns EFF/MANN PL3......
Pearn Rd EFF/MANN PL3......
Pearson Av PLYE PL4......
Pearson Rd PLYE PL4......
Peeks Av PLYMST/WEM PL9......
Peel St PLY PL1......

w Pl KEY/HAM/PCR PL2..... 16 B5
oroke La PLY PL1..... 24 A3
oroke St PLY PL4.....
os Rd PLYNW PL5..... 9 C5
air Av TOR PL11..... 22 C2
een Cl PLYNE PL6..... 5 H5
een Crs PLYNE PL6..... 5 H5
ennis Cl EFF/MANN PL3..... 17 H1
er PL11..... 22 D1
illy Av TOR PL11..... 22 D2
elly Hl PL11..... 14 D4
illy Hl TOR PL11..... 14 D4
rincess Wy PLY PL1..... 3 C4
e Gdns EFF/MANN PL3..... 16 C5
e Pk TOR PL11..... 22 C1
e Pl PLY PL4..... 17 H5
e Rd EFF/MANN PL3..... 16 C5
e Wy EFF/MANN PL3..... 16 C5
yconnequick Hl PLY PL1..... 25 E1
ycross Cl
Y/HAM/PCR PL2..... 17 F2
ycross Park Rd
PL2..... 17 E2
y's La PLYMST/WEM PL9..... 34 B1
ath Cl PLYNW PL5..... 12 D3
Gdns Vls PLYMP PL6..... 12 D3
ose St PL1..... 3 J5
ose Vis PLY PL4..... 17 H5
amar St
Y/HAM/PCR PL2..... 16 A5
inkle Cl TOR PL11..... 17 C5
ire Rd TOR PL11..... 22 D1
land Cl PLYNE PL6..... 5 H5
ire Ter PLY PL4..... 25 H1
er La PLYMST/WEM PL9..... 28 B5
lis Pl PLYNW PL5..... 11 C5
y St PLYNW PL5..... 9 H5
vinkle Dr PLYMP PL7..... 21 G4
nporth Cl PLYNW PL5..... 10 A3
rman Cl PLYMP PL7..... 20 C2
r Hopper's Hl PLYNE PL6..... 5 E1
rs Cl PLYMST/WEM PL9..... 27 H5
rsfield Cl EFF/MANN PL3..... 18 B3
rs Park Cl PLYNW PL5..... 10 A5
rs Park La PLYNE PL6..... 9 H4
ick Cl PLYNE PL6..... 5 H5
ill Cl PLYNE PL6..... 13 F3
rell Park Rd
/FF/MANN PL3.....
rell Ter EFF/MANN PL3..... 17 H4
o Cl PLYMST/WEM PL9..... 33 C1
g Gdns PLYMST/WEM PL9..... 33 F1
more St
Y/HAM/PCR PL2..... 16 B5
nix St PLY PL1..... 2 D4
Pie Dr PLY PL1..... 7 E3
La MBRK/KGSD PL10..... 37 E1
St PLY PL1..... 3 F6
im Cl KEY/HAM/PCR PL2..... 16 D4
e Salt PL12..... 8 C2
ere Dr SALT PL12..... 8 A2
wood Cl PLYMP PL7..... 20 D3
wood Dr PLYNE PL6..... 7 E4
tow Cl PLYNW PL5..... 10 A4
bure Cl PLYNW PL5..... 10 A5
sure Hl PLYMST/WEM PL9..... 27 F4
sure Hill Cl
YMST/WEM PL9..... 26 D4
ona Vw PLYMP PL7..... 20 C1
igastel Dr SALT PL12..... 8 C3
gh Gn SALT PL12..... 8 A3
er Rd PLYNE PL6..... 11 H4
sbridge Gdns PLYMP PL7..... 20 B4
sbridge La PLYNE PL6..... 12 C1
sbridge Cl PLYNE PL6.....
YNE PL6..... 13 F4
outh Rd
YMST/WEM PL9..... 19 E4
apton Hl PLYMP PL7..... 28 D1
stock Rd
YMST/WEM PL9..... 26 D5
e St PLYE PL4..... 3 K2
tree Dr PLYMP PL7..... 20 A2
Valley Path & Cycle Route
YNE PL6.....
e Dr PLYMP PL7..... 21 F5
rd Cl PLYMST/WEM PL9..... 32 B2
ards Wy SALT PL12..... 8 B3
uan Ter PLY PL1..... 2 C2
eath Gdns
Y/HAM/PCR PL2.....
phlett Cl
YMST/WEM PL9..... 26 D4
phlett Gdns
YMST/WEM PL9..... 26 D4
onby Rd EFF/MANN PL3..... 16 D5
e Park Rd PLYNW PL5..... 15 C1
ar Cl PLYMP PL7..... 21 F4
ham La PLYNW PL5..... 6 B2
eous Cl PLY PL1..... 24 D1
er Wy SALT PL12..... 8 A3
and Ct KEY/HAM/PCR PL2..... 24 B1
land Rd KEY/HAM/PCR PL2..... 24 B1
land Sq PLYE PL4..... 3 J1
land Square La North
YE PL4.....
land Vw..... 3 H1
land Vis PLYMST/WEM PL9..... 28 B5
way Cl PLYMST/WEM PL9..... 28 B5
ers Wy PLYMP PL7..... 20 B4
ery Rd PLY PL1..... 23 H1
tney Cl PLYMP PL7..... 21 G4
nds Pk SALT PL12..... 8 D3
ds St PLY PL1..... 2 B6
derham Rd EFF/MANN PL3..... 17 F2
is Gdns PLYNW PL5..... 10 D4
island Dr PLYNE PL6..... 11 H1
tonbury Cl PLYE PL6..... 6 B4
eaux Cl SALT PL12..... 8 A1
ham La KEY/HAM/PCR PL2..... 17 F2
sthood Ter
/KGSD PL10..... 30 C2

Priestley Av PLYNW PL5..... 10 A4
Primrose La PLY PL1..... 14 C5
Prince Maurice Ct PLYE PL4..... 25 H2
Prince Maurice Rd PLYE PL4..... 25 H1
Princes Rd PLYNE PL6..... 7 F5
Princess Av PLYMST/WEM PL9..... 33 E1
Princess Cl PLYNE PL6..... 10 C5
Princess Crs PLYMST/WEM PL9..... 33 E1
Princess St Ope PLY PL1..... 3 H4
Princess St PLY PL1..... 24 A2
Princess Wy PLY PL1..... 3 C4
Priory Dr PLYMP PL7..... 20 B4
Priory Lawn Ter EFF/MANN PL3..... 18 A5
Priory Ml PLYMP PL7..... 20 B4
Priory Rdg PLYMP PL7..... 20 B4
Priory Rd EFF/MANN PL3..... 18 A5
The Promenade PLY PL1..... 3 C6
Prospect La SALT PL12..... 8 A5
Prospect Pl PLY PL1..... 2 C5
Prospect Rw PLY PL1..... 24 A5
Prospect St PLYE PL4..... 3 J2
Prospect Wk SALT PL12..... 8 A5
Prouse Crs KEY/HAM/PCR PL2..... 17 E1
Prouse Ri SALT PL12..... 8 C4
Providence Pl PLY PL1..... 3 A3
Providence St PLY PL4..... 3 K1
Prynne Cl PLY PL1..... 2 E2
Pym St KEY/HAM/PCR PL2..... 24 B1

Q

Quarry Park Av
PLYMST/WEM PL9..... 26 D5
Quarry Park Rd EFF/MANN PL3..... 17 F4
PLYMST/WEM PL9..... 26 D5
Quarry St TOR PL11..... 23 C1
Quay Rd PLY PL1..... 3 J5
Queens Ct PLYNE PL6..... 7 F5
Queens Ga PLY PL1..... 2 D1
PLYE PL4.....
Queen's Gate Ms PLYE PL4..... 25 H1
Queen's Gate Villas Rd
PLYE PL4.....
Queens Rd PLYE PL4..... 25 H1
PLYNW PL5..... 10 B5
Queen St PLY PL1..... 23 H2

Richards Ter
MBRK/KGSD PL10 *..... 30 C2
Richmond Rd PLYMP PL6..... 11 H4
Richmond Wk PLY PL1..... 24 B3
The Ride PLYMST/WEM PL9..... 26 D2
Ridge Pk PLYMP PL7..... 20 C4
Ridge Park Av PLYE PL4..... 17 F5
Ridge Park Rd PLYMP PL7..... 20 C4
Ridge Rd PLYMP PL7..... 28 A1
Ridgeway PLYMP PL7..... 20 B4
SALT PL12..... 8 B5
Riga Ter EFF/MANN PL3..... 18 C5
Rigdale Cl PLYNE PL6..... 18 A2
Ringmore Wy PLYNW PL5..... 10 C3
River Ct SALT PL12 *..... 8 B1
Riverford Cl PLYMP PL7..... 6 D4
Riverside Ms SALT PL12..... 9 E5
Riverside Pl PLY PL1 *..... 23 H2
Riverside Wk PLYNW PL5..... 25 H5
The Rivers SALT PL12..... 8 B5
River Vw PLYE PL4..... 8 D3
River View La PLYE PL4..... 25 H1
Robecave Cl PLYMP PL7..... 21 G5
Robert Adams Cl PLYMP PL7..... 19 C5
Roberts Av TOR PL11..... 23 F1
Roberts Rd PLYNW PL5..... 15 G1
Robins Wy PLYMST/WEM PL9..... 27 E4
Roborough Av PLYNE PL6..... 5 F5
Roborough La PLYNE PL6..... 5 F5
Robyns Cl PLYMP PL6..... 21 F4
Rochester Rd PLY PL4..... 25 G1
Rochford Crs PLYNW PL5..... 10 B1
Rockfield Av PLYNE PL6..... 5 E5
Rock Gdns PLYMST/WEM PL9..... 26 D3
Rockhill PLYNW PL5..... 5 E5
Rockingham Rd EFF/MANN PL3..... 18 A4
Rockville Pk PLYMST/WEM PL9..... 27 E4
Rockwood Rd PLYNE PL6..... 7 E5
Rocky Park Av
PLYMST/WEM PL9..... 27 E4
Rocky Park Rd
PLYMST/WEM PL9..... 27 E5
Roddick Wy PLYMP PL7..... 21 G4
Rodney St PLYNW PL5..... 15 H1
Roeselare Av TOR PL11..... 23 E1
Roeselare Cl TOR PL11..... 23 E1
Rogate Dr PLYNE PL6..... 12 D2
Rogers Dr SALT PL12..... 8 B2
Rolle St PLYMST/WEM PL9..... 26 C4
Rollis Park Rd
PLYMST/WEM PL9..... 26 C4
Rolston Cl PLYNW PL5..... 5 E5
Roman Rd PLYNW PL5..... 10 A5
Roman Wy PLYNW PL5..... 10 A4
Romilly Gdns PLYMP PL7..... 19 H4
Romney Cl PLYNW PL5..... 10 D5
Ronald Ter KEY/HAM/PCR PL2..... 16 B4
Ronsdale Cl EFF/MANN PL3..... 18 A4
Roope Cl PLYNW PL5..... 15 G2
Roper Av PLYMST/WEM PL9..... 26 D4
Rorkes Cl PLYNW PL5..... 10 A4
Rosebery Av PLYE PL4..... 26 A1
Rosebery Rd PLYE PL4..... 26 A1
Rosedale Av KEY/HAM/PCR PL2..... 17 E2
Rosedean Ct EFF/MANN PL3..... 17 H3
Rosedown Av
KEY/HAM/PCR PL2..... 16 C2
Rose Gdns PLYNE PL6..... 12 D1
Rose Hl PLYMST/WEM PL9..... 39 G4
Rosehip Cl PLYNE PL6..... 7 E4
Rosevean Gdns PLYMST/WEM PL9..... 17 H3
Roseveare Cl PLYMST/WEM PL9..... 27 G5
Rosewood Cl PLYMST/WEM PL9..... 33 F2
Rospeath Crs
PLYMST/WEM PL9..... 27 F1
Rosslyn Park Rd
PLYMST/WEM PL9..... 39 C3
Ross St KEY/HAM/PCR PL2..... 16 A5
Rothbury Cl PLYNE PL6..... 13 E2
Rothbury Gdns PLYNE PL6..... 13 D2
Rothesay Gdns PLYNW PL5..... 11 E3
Rougemont Cl EFF/MANN PL3..... 18 B2
Rowan Cl EFF/MANN PL3..... 18 A3
Rowan Ct SALT PL12..... 8 A4
Rowan Wy PLYNE PL6..... 7 E4
Rowden St EFF/MANN PL3..... 17 G4
Rowdown Cl PLYMP PL7..... 21 H5
Rowe St TOR PL11..... 23 F1
Rowland Cl PLYMST/WEM PL9..... 33 E2
Row La PLYNW PL5..... 10 A4
Royal Navy Av
KEY/HAM/PCR PL2..... 16 A4
Royal Pde PLY PL1..... 3 G4
Royal William Rd PLY PL1..... 2 B7
Rudyerd Wk EFF/MANN PL3..... 18 C5
Rufford Cl KEY/HAM/PCR PL2..... 16 C2
Ruskin Crs PLYMP PL7..... 11 F4
Russell Av PLYNW PL5..... 11 E5
Russell Cl PLYMST/WEM PL9..... 27 H5
SALT PL12..... 8 C5
Russell Pl PLYE PL4..... 25 E1
Russet Wd PLYNW PL5..... 10 B2
Rutger Pl PLY PL4..... 24 D1
Ruthven Cl PLYNE PL6..... 17 H1
Rutland Rd PLY PL4..... 17 G5
Rydal Cl PLYNE PL6..... 12 D4
Ryder Rd KEY/HAM/PCR PL2..... 16 B5
Rye Hl SALT PL12..... 8 D5
Ryeland Cl PLYMST/WEM PL9..... 39 H1

S

St Andrews Cl SALT PL12..... 8 A4
St Andrews Cross PLY PL1..... 3 H5
St Andrew's Pl
MBRK/KGSD PL10..... 37 E1
St Andrew's St
MBRK/KGSD PL10..... 37 E1
PLY PL1..... 3 H4
St Andrew St MBRK/KGSD PL10..... 30 B2

St Anne's Rd PLYNE PL6..... 6 D5
St Aubyn Av KEY/HAM/PCR PL2..... 16 B4
St Aubyn Rd PLY PL1..... 24 A2
St Aubyn St PLY PL1..... 24 A2
St Barnabas Ter PLY PL1..... 2 D1
St Boniface Cl
KEY/HAM/PCR PL2..... 17 E2
St Bridget Av PLYNE PL6..... 17 H1
St Dunstan's Ter PLYE PL4..... 26 A2
St Edward Gdns PLYNE PL6..... 12 B5
St Elizabeth Cl PLYMP PL7..... 28 D1
St Erth Rd KEY/HAM/PCR PL2..... 17 F1
St Eval Pl PLYNW PL5..... 10 A2
St Francis Ct PLYNW PL5..... 10 C5
St Gabriel's Av EFF/MANN PL3..... 17 F4
St George's Av
KEY/HAM/PCR PL2..... 17 E2
St Georges Rd SALT PL12..... 8 C3
St George's Ter
KEY/HAM/PCR PL2..... 16 B5
St Hilary Ter PLYE PL4..... 26 A2
St James Ct TOR PL11 *..... 23 F1
St James' Pl East PLY PL1..... 3 F5
St James' Pl West PLY PL1..... 3 F5
St James Rd TOR PL11..... 23 F1
St John's Bridge Rd PLYE PL4..... 25 H3
St John's Cl MBRK/KGSD PL10..... 30 C2
PLYMP PL6..... 12 D1
St John's Dr PLYMST/WEM PL9..... 32 B1
St John's Rd MBRK/KGSD PL10..... 30 C1
PLYE PL4.....
PLYMST/WEM PL9..... 32 A1
St John's St PLYE PL4..... 25 H3
St Johns Yd PLYE PL4 *..... 25 H3
St Joseph's Cl PLYNE PL6..... 11 H5
St Jude's Rd PLYE PL4..... 25 H5
St Keverne Pl
PLYMST/WEM PL9..... 17 F1
St Lawrence Rd PLY PL4..... 25 C1
St Leonard's Rd PLYE PL4..... 26 A2
St Leo Pl KEY/HAM/PCR PL2..... 16 A5
St Levan Rd KEY/HAM/PCR PL2..... 16 C4
St Margarets Rd PLYMP PL7..... 19 G3
St Marks Rd PLYNE PL6..... 12 C2
St Martin's Av EFF/MANN PL3..... 17 F2
St Marys Cl PLYMP PL7..... 20 A3
St Marys Ct PLYMP PL7..... 20 B3
St Mary's Rd PLYMP PL7..... 19 H3
St Mary St PLY PL1..... 2 C3
St Maurice Ms PLYMP PL7..... 20 C5
St Maurice Rd PLYMP PL7..... 28 D1
St Maurice Vw PLYMP PL7..... 21 F5
St Michael Av
KEY/HAM/PCR PL2..... 16 B4
St Michael's Cl PLYMP PL7..... 24 A3
St Michael's Ter PLY PL1..... 24 B1
PLYE PL4.....
St Modwen Rd PLYNE PL6..... 19 E2
St Nazaire Ap PLY PL1..... 24 B2
St Nazaire Cl PLY PL1..... 24 A2
St Pancras Av PLYNW PL5..... 10 B2
St Pauls Cl EFF/MANN PL3..... 18 C4
St Paul St PLY PL1..... 2 B6
St Peter Cl PLYMP PL7..... 20 D5
St Peters Rd PLYNW PL5..... 11 F4
St Simon's La PLYE PL4..... 26 B1
St Stephen Rd PLYMP PL7..... 28 D1
St Stephen's Hl SALT PL12..... 8 A5
St Stephens Pl PLYMP PL7 *..... 28 C4
St Stephens Rd SALT PL12..... 8 C4
St Stephen St PLY PL1 *..... 24 B3
St Thomas Cl PLYMP PL7..... 28 D1
St Vincent St
KEY/HAM/PCR PL2..... 16 A5
St Werburgh Cl
PLYMST/WEM PL9..... 39 G4
Salamanca St TOR PL11..... 23 F1
Salcombe Rd PLYE PL4..... 25 H1
Salisbury Ope
KEY/HAM/PCR PL2..... 16 D4
Salisbury Rd PLYE PL4..... 26 A1
Saltash Rd KEY/HAM/PCR PL2..... 15 H4
PLYE PL4.....
PLYNW PL5..... 16 A3
Saltburn Rd PLYNW PL5..... 9 G4
Salt Ml SALT PL12..... 8 D2
Sandford Rd PLYMST/WEM PL9..... 27 F4
Sandon Wk PLYNE PL6..... 12 C5
Sandy Rd PLYMP PL7..... 21 G5
Sango Ct MBRK/KGSD PL10..... 30 D1
Sango Rd TOR PL11..... 23 E2
Sarum Cl EFF/MANN PL3..... 17 H2
Savage Rd PLYNW PL5..... 15 G1
Sawrey St PLY PL1..... 2 A3
School Ct PLYMP PL7..... 20 B2
School Dr PLYMP PL7..... 20 B2
School La PLYMP PL7..... 20 C5
Sconner Rd TOR PL11..... 23 E1
Scott Av PLYNW PL5..... 11 G5
Scott Rd KEY/HAM/PCR PL2..... 16 D4
Seacroft Rd PLYNW PL5..... 15 G1
Seaton La PLYE PL4..... 17 G5
Seaton Pl KEY/HAM/PCR PL2..... 16 B4
Sea View Av PLYE PL4..... 26 A1
Sea View Dr PLYMST/WEM PL9..... 39 G3
Sea View Ter PLYE PL4..... 25 H1
Second Av PLY PL1..... 2 A3
PLYMST/WEM PL9..... 26 A2
Sedley Wy PLYNW PL5..... 11 F3
Sefton Av PLYE PL4..... 18 A5
Sefton Cl PLYE PL4..... 26 A1
Segrave Rd KEY/HAM/PCR PL2..... 16 D4
Selkirk Pl PLYNW PL5..... 11 G4
Sellon Ct PLY PL1..... 8 E3
Selsden Cl PLYMST/WEM PL9..... 34 H1
Sendall's Wy PLYNE PL6..... 11 H3
Sennen Cl PLYNE PL6..... 14 D5
Sennen Pl KEY/HAM/PCR PL2..... 16 A4
Serpell Cl PLYNE PL6..... 5 C5
Seven Stars La PLYNW PL5..... 4 D5
Seven Trees Ct PLYE PL4..... 25 H1

Severn Pl EFF/MANN PL3..... 18 C4
Seymour Av PLYE PL4..... 26 A1
Seymour Dr EFF/MANN PL3..... 17 H4
Seymour Ms PLY PL4..... 26 A1
Seymour Pk EFF/MANN PL3..... 18 A4
Seymour Pk EFF/MANN PL3..... 17 H4
Seymour Rd PLY PL4..... 19 H5
Shaftesbury Cottages PLYE PL4..... 3 K1
Shakespeare Rd PLYNW PL5..... 10 D4
Shaldon Crs PLYNW PL5..... 10 D5
Shallowford Cl PLYNE PL6..... 18 C1
Shallowford Rd PLYNE PL6..... 18 C1
Shapleys Gdns
PLYMST/WEM PL9..... 33 G2
Shapters Rd PLYE PL4..... 26 A3
Shapters Wy PLYE PL4..... 26 B4
Sharon Wy PLYNE PL6..... 12 A1
Sharrose Rd EFF/MANN PL3..... 32 B2
Shaw Wy PLYMST/WEM PL9..... 26 A5
Shearwood Cl PLYMP PL7..... 20 A3
Sheepstor Rd PLYMP PL7..... 12 D5
Shell Cl PLYNE PL6..... 13 E5
Shelley Wy PLYMP PL7..... 5 H5
Shepherd's La PLYE PL4..... 25 H5
Sherborne Cl PLYMST/WEM PL9..... 34 A1
Sherford Crs PLYMST/WEM PL9..... 28 A5
PLYNW PL5..... 10 B5
Sherford Rd EFF/MANN PL3..... 18 B3
Sherford Wk PLYMST/WEM PL9..... 28 C5
Sheridan Rd PLYNW PL5..... 11 E5
Sherril Cl PLYMST/WEM PL9..... 33 F3
Sherwell La PLYE PL4..... 3 J1
Shipley Wk PLYNE PL6..... 12 C5
Shirburn Rd PLYNE PL6..... 12 B5
Shirley Gdns PLYNW PL5..... 11 E5
Short Park Rd EFF/MANN PL3..... 17 F4
Shortwood Crs
PLYMST/WEM PL9..... 27 G5
Shrewsbury Rd PLYNW PL5..... 10 D2
Shute Park Rd
PLYMST/WEM PL9..... 33 F1
Silver Birch Cl PLYNE PL6..... 6 C4
Silver Stream Wy YLMP PL8..... 35 F2
Silver St SALT PL12..... 8 E4
Silver Ter MBRK/KGSD PL10..... 31 E1
Simon Cl PLYMST/WEM PL9..... 33 E1
Sithney St PLYNW PL5..... 9 G5
Skardale Gdns PLYNE PL6..... 18 D1
Skardon Pl PLYE PL4..... 3 J1
Skerries Rd PLYNE PL6..... 5 H4
Skylark Ri PLYNE PL6..... 7 E5
Slade Cl PLYMST/WEM PL9..... 33 G2
Slatelands Cl PLYMP PL7..... 29 F1
Smallack Cl PLYNE PL6..... 11 H4
Smallack Dr PLYNE PL6..... 11 H4
Smallridge Cl PLYMST/WEM PL9..... 33 F2
Smeaton Sq PLYNE PL6..... 18 D3
Smithy Cl SALT PL12..... 8 A2
Smockpark La
PLYMST/WEM PL9..... 38 C4
Somerset Place La
EFF/MANN PL3..... 16 C5
South Down Rd
KEY/HAM/PCR PL2..... 16 D3
Southdown Rd
MBRK/KGSD PL10..... 30 D1
South Down Ter
MBRK/KGSD PL10..... 31 E1
Southern Cl KEY/HAM/PCR PL2..... 16 A2
Southern Ter PLYE PL4..... 17 H5
Southernway
PLYMST/WEM PL9..... 27 G4
Southgate Av
PLYMST/WEM PL9..... 33 E3
Southgate Cl
PLYMST/WEM PL9..... 33 E3
South Hl PLY PL1..... 2 A1
PLYMST/WEM PL9..... 33 C2
Southland Park Crs
PLYMST/WEM PL9..... 39 C3
Southland Park Rd
PLYMST/WEM PL9..... 39 G4
Southside St PLY PL1..... 3 J5
Southview Wk MBRK/KGSD PL10..... 31 E1
South Vw PLYMST/WEM PL9..... 27 H5
South View Cl PLYMP PL7..... 20 B2
South View Pk PLYMP PL7..... 20 B2
South View Ter PLYE PL4..... 26 A2
Southway Dr PLYNE PL6..... 11 F1
Southway La PLYNE PL6..... 6 B4
Southwell Rd PLYNE PL6..... 11 H5
South West Coast Pth
MBRK/KGSD PL10..... 36 C2
PLYMST/WEM PL9..... 32 A1
Sparke Cl PLYMP PL7..... 19 G5
The Speares SALT PL12..... 8 A4
Speedwell Cl MBRK/KGSD PL10..... 30 D2
Speedwell Crs PLYNE PL6..... 18 A2
Spencer Gdns SALT PL12..... 8 C5
Spencer Rd PLYMST/WEM PL9..... 27 F4
The Spinney PLYMP PL7..... 21 E5
Spire Ct EFF/MANN PL3..... 18 B3
Spire Hill Pk SALT PL12..... 8 A4
Springfield Av
PLYMST/WEM PL9..... 33 G1
Springfield Cl
PLYMST/WEM PL9..... 27 H5
Springfield Dr EFF/MANN PL3..... 16 C5
Springfield La
PLYMST/WEM PL9..... 27 H5
Springfield Ri
PLYMST/WEM PL9..... 27 H5
Springfield Rd
PLYMST/WEM PL9..... 33 H1
Springhill KEY/HAM/PCR PL2..... 17 E1
Springhill Gn
KEY/HAM/PCR PL2..... 17 E1
Spring Pk PLYNE PL6..... 7 E4
Spring Rd PLYMST/WEM PL9..... 38 C5
Springwood Cl PLYMP PL7..... 29 E1
Spruce Gdns PLYMP PL7..... 21 F4
The Square PLY PL1..... 2 C3
SALT PL12 *..... 8 A3

Staddiscombe Rd
PLYMST/WEM PL9 33 F4
Staddon Crs *PLYMST/WEM* PL9 33 E1
Staddon Gn *PLYMST/WEM* PL9 32 D1
Staddon La *PLYMST/WEM* PL9 32 A3
Staddon Park Rd
PLYMST/WEM PL9 33 E1
Staddon Terrace La *PLY* PL1 3 F1
Stag La *PLYMST/WEM* PL9 27 H3
Stamford Cl *PLYMST/WEM* PL9 32 A1
Stamford La *PLYMST/WEM* PL9 32 A2
Stamps Hl *YLMP* PL8 35 E1
Stanborough Rd
PLYMST/WEM PL9 27 F5
Stanbury Av *PLYNE* PL6 11 H5
Standarhay Cl
PLYMST/WEM PL9 28 A5
Standarhay Vls
PLYMST/WEM PL9 28 A5
Stangray Av *PLYE* PL4 17 F5
Stanhope Rd *PLYNW* PL5 9 G4
Stanlake Cl *SALT* PL12 * 8 B4
Stanley Pl *PLYE* PL4 26 B2
Staple Cl *PLYNE* PL6 6 C3
Stapleford Gdns *PLYNW* PL5 10 B1
Station Rd *KEY/HAM/PCR* PL2 16 A4
PLYMP PL7 20 B3
PLYMST/WEM PL9 28 A5
PLYNW PL5 4 C5
Steeple Cl *PLYMST/WEM* PL9 33 F3
Steer Park Rd *PLYMP* PL7 21 G4
Steer Point Rd *YLMP* PL8 34 D4
Stefan Cl *PLYMST/WEM* PL9 32 B2
Stenlake Pl *PLYE* PL4 26 B2
Stenlake Ter *PLYE* PL4 26 B2
Stentaway Cl
PLYMST/WEM PL9 27 F4
Stentaway Dr
PLYMST/WEM PL9 27 F4
Stentaway Rd
PLYMST/WEM PL9 27 F5
Stillman St *PLYE* PL4 3 J4
Stirling Ct *PLYNW* PL5 9 G5
Stirling Rd *PLYNW* PL5 9 G5
Stoggy La *PLYMP* PL7 21 F3
Stoke Rd *PLY* PL1 2 D2
Stokes La *PLY* PL1 3 J5
Stokingway Cl
PLYMST/WEM PL9 33 E2
Stone Barton Cl *PLYMP* PL7 20 A3
Stonebarton Cl *PLYMP* PL7 20 A3
Stone Barton Rd *PLYMP* PL7 20 A3
Stonehouse Barracks *PLY* PL1 2 B5
Stonehouse Br *PLY* PL1 2 A4
Stonehouse St *PLY* PL1 2 B4
Stopford Pl *PLY* PL1 24 B1
Stott Cl *EFF/MANN* PL3 18 D4
Stour Cl *EFF/MANN* PL3 18 D3
Stowe Gdns *PLYNW* PL5 10 D4
Strand St *PLY* PL1 2 A6
Strode Rd *PLYMP* PL7 20 D3
Stroma Cl *PLYNE* PL6 5 H4
Stroud Park Rd
KEY/HAM/PCR PL2 17 E2
Stuart Rd *PLY* PL1 2 B1
Sturdee Rd *KEY/HAM/PCR* PL2 16 C4
Summerfields *SALT* PL12 8 A5
Summerlands Cl *PLYMP* PL7 21 G4
Summerlands Gdns *PLYMP* PL7 21 G4
Summers Cl *PLYNE* PL6 18 B2
Sunderland Cl
PLYMST/WEM PL9 32 A1
Sunningdale Rd *SALT* PL12 8 B4
Sunny Dene *PLYNW* PL5 9 H5
Sunnyside *PLYMST/WEM* PL9 * 26 A5
Sunnyside Rd *PLYE* PL4 26 B2
Sussex Pl *PLY* PL1 3 H5
Sussex Rd *KEY/HAM/PCR* PL2 16 B4
Sussex St *PLY* PL1 3 H5
Sussex Ter *KEY/HAM/PCR* PL2 16 B4
Sutherland Rd *PLYE* PL4 25 F1
Sutton Rd *PLYE* PL4 25 H3
Swaindale Rd *EFF/MANN* PL3 17 G3
Swale Cl *EFF/MANN* PL3 18 B3
Swallows End
PLYMST/WEM PL9 27 E4
Swan Cl *MBRK/KGSD* PL10 31 E1
Swan Gdns *PLYMP* PL7 20 D4
Swinburne Gdns *PLYNW* PL5 10 D5
Sycamore Av *PLYE* PL4 26 A3
Sycamore Dr *PLYNE* PL6 6 C4
TOR PL11 22 D1
Sycamore Wy *PLYNE* PL6 13 E1
Sydney Cl *PLYMP* PL7 20 C5
Sydney Rd *TOR* PL11 23 E1
Sydney St *PLY* PL1 3 F1
Sylvan Ct *PLY* PL1 2 B1
Symons Rd *SALT* PL12 8 D4

T

Tailyour Rd *PLYNE* PL6 11 H4
Talbot Gdns *PLYNW* PL5 15 G2
Tamar Av *KEY/HAM/PCR* PL2 16 A4
Tamar Br *PLYNW* PL5 9 F4
Tamar St *KEY/HAM/PCR* PL2 24 A1
SALT PL12 9 E4
Tamar Ter *SALT* PL12 9 E4
Tamar Vls *PLYMST/WEM* PL9 26 D5
Tamar Whf *KEY/HAM/PCR* PL2 23 H1
Tamerton Av *PLYNW* PL5 9 H5
Tamerton Cl *PLYNW* PL5 4 C5
Tamerton Foliot Rd *PLYNW* PL5 4 D5
Tamerton Rd *PLYNE* PL6 6 C1
Tangmere Av *PLYNW* PL5 10 A1
Tannery Ct *SALT* PL12 8 A4
Tapp's La *YLMP* PL8 35 F2
Tapson Dr *PLYMST/WEM* PL9 32 A1
Taunton Av *PLYNW* PL5 10 D1
Tavistock Pl *PLYE* PL4 3 J2
Tavistock Rd *PLYNE* PL6 6 B5
PLYNE PL6 17 G1
Tavy Pl *PLYE* PL4 17 H5
Tavy Rd *SALT* PL12 9 E3
Taw Cl *EFF/MANN* PL3 18 D3
Tay Gdns *PLYNE* PL6 18 D2
Taylor Rd *SALT* PL12 8 A3
Teats Hill Rd *PLYE* PL4 25 H4
Tees Cl *EFF/MANN* PL3 18 C2
Teign Rd *EFF/MANN* PL3 18 B3
Telegraph Whf *PLY* PL1 2 A6
Telford Crs *PLYNW* PL5 10 B4
Temeraire Rd *PLYNW* PL5 11 F4
Tenby Rd *PLYNW* PL5 9 G5
Tern Gdns *PLYMP* PL7 20 D4
Tewkesbury Cl
KEY/HAM/PCR PL2 16 C1
Thackeray Gdns *PLYNW* PL5 10 D5
Thames Gdns *EFF/MANN* PL3 18 D4
Thanckes Dr *TOR* PL11 23 E1
Theatre Ope *PLY* PL1 24 B3
Therlow Rd *EFF/MANN* PL3 18 B3
Thetford Gdns *PLYNE* PL6 18 D1
Third Av *KEY/HAM/PCR* PL2 16 A2
PLY PL1 2 A3
PLYMST/WEM PL9 27 G3
Thirlmere Gdns *PLYNE* PL6 11 H2
Thistle Cl *PLYNE* PL6 7 E4
Thornbury Park Av
EFF/MANN PL3 17 F3
Thornbury Rd *PLYNE* PL6 13 E2
Thornhill Rd *EFF/MANN* PL3 17 G3
Thornhill Wy *EFF/MANN* PL3 17 G3
Thorn La *SALT* PL12 8 A3
Thorn Pk *EFF/MANN* PL3 17 G4
Thornton Av *PLYE* PL4 25 H1
Thornville Ter
PLYMST/WEM PL9 26 C5
Thornyville Cl
PLYMST/WEM PL9 26 C4
Thornyville Dr
PLYMST/WEM PL9 26 C5
Thornyville Vls
PLYMST/WEM PL9 26 C5
Thurlestone Wk *PLYNE* PL6 12 D5
Tillard Cl *PLYMP* PL7 21 G4
Tilly Cl *PLYMST/WEM* PL9 33 F3
Tincombe *SALT* PL12 8 A4
Tin La *PLYE* PL4 3 K4
Tintagel Crs *KEY/HAM/PCR* PL2 17 E1
Tintern Av *PLYE* PL4 26 A3
Tithe Rd *PLYMP* PL7 19 G2
Tiverton Cl *PLYNE* PL6 6 B3
Tobruk Rd *SALT* PL12 8 C3
Tollox Pl *EFF/MANN* PL3 18 B5
Torbridge *PLYMP* PL7 20 C2
Torbridge Cl *SALT* PL12 8 B4
Torbryan Cl *PLYNE* PL6 19 E1
Tor Cl *EFF/MANN* PL3 19 E3
Torland Rd *EFF/MANN* PL3 17 G2
Torr Crs *EFF/MANN* PL3 17 G2
Torridge Cl *PLYMP* PL7 21 E3
Torridge Rd *PLYMP* PL7 20 D3
Torridge Wy *EFF/MANN* PL3 18 C4
Torr La *EFF/MANN* PL3 17 G2
Tor Rd *EFF/MANN* PL3 17 G2
Torr View Av *EFF/MANN* PL3 17 F2
Torver Cl *PLYNE* PL6 12 D4
Tory Brook Av *PLYMP* PL7 20 C3
Tory Brook Ct *PLYMP* PL7 20 C3
Tory Wy *PLYMP* PL7 20 B3
Tothill Av *PLYE* PL4 25 H2
Tothill Rd *PLYE* PL4 25 H2
Totnes Cl *PLYMP* PL7 21 F5
Tower Ct *SALT* PL12 8 A4
Towerfield Dr *PLYNE* PL6 6 C3
Towers Cl *PLYNE* PL6 13 F4
Tower Vw *SALT* PL12 8 B5
Townshend Av
KEY/HAM/PCR PL2 16 A4
Tracey Ct *PLY* PL1 3 F2
Trafalgar Cl *PLYNW* PL5 15 H1
Trafalgar Place La *PLY* PL1 24 B1
Trafalgar St *PLYE* PL4 3 K3
Traine Brake *PLYMST/WEM* PL9 34 A5
Traine Rd *PLYMST/WEM* PL9 39 H1
Tramway Rd *PLYNE* PL6 6 D4
Transit Wy *PLYNW* PL5 11 E3
Treago Gdns *PLYNE* PL6 6 C3
Treby Rd *PLYMP* PL7 20 D5
Treetop Cl *SALT* PL12 8 B2
Trefusis Gdns *EFF/MANN* PL3 18 A5
Trefusis Ter *MBRK/KGSD* PL10 30 C1
Tregenna Cl *PLYMP* PL7 21 G5
Tregoning Rd *TOR* PL11 22 D2
Trehill La *MBRK/KGSD* PL10 36 C2
Trelawney Av *PLYNW* PL5 9 H5
Trelawney Cl *TOR* PL11 22 C1
Trelawney Pl *PLYNW* PL5 9 H5
Trelawney Ri *TOR* PL11 22 C1
Trelawney Rd *EFF/MANN* PL3 17 F4
SALT PL12 8 C4
Trelawney Wy *TOR* PL11 22 C1
Trelawny Rd *PLYMP* PL7 20 A3
Treloweth Cl
KEY/HAM/PCR PL2 17 F1
Trematon Cl *TOR* PL11 14 C5
Trematon Ter *PLYE* PL4 17 G5
Trencher La *MBRK/KGSD* PL10 30 B5
Trendlewood Rd *PLYNE* PL6 6 D4
Trengrouse Av *TOR* PL11 22 D1
Trent Cl *EFF/MANN* PL3 18 B3
Trentham Cl *PLYNE* PL6 6 B5
Tresillian St *PLYE* PL4 26 A3
Tresluggan Rd *PLYNW* PL5 9 H5
Tretower Cl *PLYNE* PL6 11 H1
Trevannion Cl *PLYNE* PL6 18 A1
Treveneague Gdns
KEY/HAM/PCR PL2 17 F1
Treverbyn Cl *PLYMP* PL7 20 B3
Treverbyn Rd *PLYMP* PL7 20 B3
Trevessa Cl *KEY/HAM/PCR* PL2 17 F1
Trevithick Av *TOR* PL11 14 C5
Trevithick Rd *PLYNW* PL5 10 A5
Trevol Pl *TOR* PL11 22 C1
Trevol Rd *TOR* PL11 22 A1
Trevone Gdns *PLYNW* PL5 17 F1
Trevorder Cl *TOR* PL11 22 D2
Trevorder Rd *TOR* PL11 22 D2
Trevose Wy *EFF/MANN* PL3 18 C3
Trewithy Dr *PLYNE* PL6 11 H5
Trowbridge Cl *PLYNW* PL5 11 E2
Truro Dr *PLYNW* PL5 10 C1
Tucker Cl *KEY/HAM/PCR* PL2 16 B1
Tudor Cl *PLYMST/WEM* PL9 33 E3
Turbill Gdns *PLYMP* PL7 21 F4
Turnquay *PLYMST/WEM* PL9 26 B5
Turret Gv *PLYE* PL4 17 H5
Tuxton Cl *PLYMP* PL7 29 F1
Two Hills Pk *SALT* PL12 8 A4
Tyiney Cl *PLYNE* PL6 6 B5
Tyndale Cl *PLYNW* PL5 10 D5
Tything Wk *EFF/MANN* PL3 17 G3

U

Ullswater Crs *PLYNE* PL6 11 G2
Undercliff Rd
PLYMST/WEM PL9 26 B5
Underhill Rd *EFF/MANN* PL3 16 C5
Underlane *PLYMP* PL7 20 A4
PLYMST/WEM PL9 33 E1
Underwood Rd *PLYMP* PL7 20 B5
Unicorn Cl *PLYMP* PL7 19 H3
Union Pl *PLY* PL1 2 D4
Union St *PLY* PL1 2 C4
Unity Cl *PLYNE* PL6 12 D1
Upland Dr *PLYNE* PL6 11 H1
Upland Gdns *PLYMST/WEM* PL9 39 H2
Uplands *SALT* PL12 8 C5
Upper Ridings *PLYMP* PL7 21 F2
Upton Cl *EFF/MANN* PL3 18 B2
Uxbridge Dr *PLYNW* PL5 10 A2

V

Vaagso Cl *PLY* PL1 24 A2
Valiant Av *PLYNW* PL5 10 C2
Valletort La *PLY* PL1 2 B1
Valletort Pl *PLY* PL1 2 B3
Valletort Rd *EFF/MANN* PL3 24 C1
Valley Dr *PLYMST/WEM* PL9 39 G3
Valley Rd *PLYMP* PL7 19 H4
SALT PL12 8 C4
Valley Vw *PLYNE* PL6 6 D4
Valley View Cl *EFF/MANN* PL3 18 B3
Valley View Rd *EFF/MANN* PL3 18 B2
Valley Wk *PLYNE* PL6 6 D5
Vanguard Cl *PLYNW* PL5 11 F5
Vapron Rd *EFF/MANN* PL3 17 G3
Vauban Pl *KEY/HAM/PCR* PL2 16 B5
Vaughan Cl *KEY/HAM/PCR* PL2 17 E2
Vauxhall St *PLY* PL1 3 F4
Veasypark *PLYMST/WEM* PL9 39 H3
Venn Ct *EFF/MANN* PL3 17 G3
Venn Crs *EFF/MANN* PL3 17 G3
Venn Dr *YLMP* PL8 35 E3
Venn Gdns *EFF/MANN* PL3 17 G2
Venn Gv *EFF/MANN* PL3 17 G2
Venn Wy *EFF/MANN* PL3 17 G2
Vermont Gdns
KEY/HAM/PCR PL2 16 B2
Verna Pl *PLYNW* PL5 9 H4
Verna Rd *PLYNW* PL5 9 H4
Vicarage Gdns *PLYNW* PL5 9 F5
Vicarage Rd *PLYMP* PL7 20 A4
TOR PL11 23 F2
Victoria Av *PLY* PL1 2 D1
Victoria Pl *KEY/HAM/PCR* PL2 16 B5
PLY PL1 2 C5
Victoria Rd *PLYNW* PL5 9 H5
SALT PL12 8 D4
Victoria St *TOR* PL11 23 F1
Victory St *KEY/HAM/PCR* PL2 16 A3
Village Dr *PLYNE* PL6 6 C2
Villiers Cl *PLYMST/WEM* PL9 26 D5
Vincent Wy *SALT* PL12 8 D4
Vine Crs *KEY/HAM/PCR* PL2 16 D3
Vine Gdns *KEY/HAM/PCR* PL2 16 D3
Vinery La *PLYMST/WEM* PL9 28 B4
Vinstone Wy *PLYNW* PL5 9 H5
Violet Dr *PLYNE* PL6 7 E3
Virginia Gdns
KEY/HAM/PCR PL2 16 B2

W

Waddon Cl *PLYMP* PL7 20 C2
Waggon Hl *PLYMP* PL7 21 E5
Wain Pk *PLYMP* PL7 20 D5
Wakefield Av *PLYNW* PL5 * 9 H4
Wake St *EFF/MANN* PL3 25 E1
Walcot Cl *PLYNE* PL6 13 E3
Waldon Cl *PLYMP* PL7 21 F3
Walker Ter *PLY* PL1 2 E6
Walkhampton Wk *PLYNE* PL6 13 E5
Wallace Rd *PLYMP* PL7 21 E5
Wallpark Cl *PLYMP* PL7 20 D2
Walnut Cl *PLYMP* PL7 21 F4
Walnut Dr *PLYMP* PL7 21 G4
Walnut Gdns *PLYMP* PL7 21 G4
Walsingham Ct *PLYMP* PL7 21 F4
Walters Rd *PLYNW* PL5 9 G4
Waltham Pl *KEY/HAM/PCR* PL2 16 C1
Walton Crs *PLYNW* PL5 11 E5
Wandle Pl *EFF/MANN* PL3 18 D4
Wanstead Gv *PLYNW* PL5 10 C3
Wantage Gdns *PLY* PL1 2 D2
Warburton Gdns *PLYNW* PL5 9 G5
Wardlow Cl *PLYNE* PL6 17 H1
Wardlow Gdns *PLYNE* PL6 17 H1
Ward Pl *EFF/MANN* PL3 18 B4
Warfelton Crs *SALT* PL12 8 C4
Warfelton Gdns *SALT* PL12 8 C4
Warfelton Ter *SALT* PL12 8 C3
Waring Rd *PLYNE* PL6 5 F4
Warleigh Av *KEY/HAM/PCR* PL2 16 A4
Warleigh Crs *PLYNE* PL6 11 G1
Warleigh Rd *PLYE* PL4 17 G5
Warmwell Rd *PLYNW* PL5 10 A2
Warraton Cl *SALT* PL12 8 B3
Warraton Gn *SALT* PL12 * 8 B3
Warraton Rd *SALT* PL12 8 B3
Warren Cl *PLYMST/WEM* PL9 39 G4
Warren La *PLYNW* PL5 4 C3
Warren Pk *PLYNE* PL6 6 D4
Warren St *KEY/HAM/PCR* PL2 16 A5
Warspite Gdns *PLYNW* PL5 11 F4
Warton Cl *PLYNW* PL5 11 F4
Warwick Av *PLYNW* PL5 11 F2
Warwick Orchard Cl
PLYNW PL5 10 D3
Wasdale Cl *PLYNE* PL6 12 D4
Wasdale Gdns *PLYNE* PL6 12 D4
Washbourne Cl *PLY* PL1 24 A1
Waterloo Cl *PLY* PL1 2 B3
Waterloo St *PLY* PL1 24 B1
PLYE PL4 3 K1
Watson Pl *PLYE* PL4 25 H2
Watts Park Rd
KEY/HAM/PCR PL2 17 E2
Watts' Rd *PLYE* PL4 26 A2
Waveney Gdns *PLYNW* PL5 11 E3
Waverley Rd *PLYNW* PL5 9 H4
Wavish Pk *TOR* PL11 22 C1
Wearde Rd *SALT* PL12 14 C1
Weir Cl *PLYNE* PL6 13 F4
Weir Gdns *PLYNE* PL6 13 F4
Weir Rd *PLYNE* PL6 13 E3
Welbeck Av *PLYE* PL4 25 F1
Wellfield Cl *PLYMP* PL7 21 G4
Well Gdns *PLY* PL1 3 F2
Wellhay Cl *PLYMST/WEM* PL9 34 A1
Wellington St *PLY* PL1 2 A1
PLYE PL4 3 K1
TOR PL11 23 F2
Well Park Rd *TOR* PL11 23 F1
Wellsbourne Pk *EFF/MANN* PL3 18 A3
Wells Ct *MBRK/KGSD* PL10 30 C3
Welman Rd *MBRK/KGSD* PL10 30 D1
Welsford Av *KEY/HAM/PCR* PL2 16 B4
Wembury Meadow
PLYMST/WEM PL9 39 H3
Wembury Park Rd
EFF/MANN PL3 17 F3
Wembury Rd
PLYMST/WEM PL9 33 G3
Wenlock Gdns
KEY/HAM/PCR PL2 16 D1
Wensum Cl *PLYMP* PL7 21 E5
Wentwood Gdns *PLYNE* PL6 13 E3
Wentwood Pl *PLYNE* PL6 13 E3
Wentworth Pl *PLYE* PL4 26 B2
Wentworth Wy *SALT* PL12 8 A4
Wesley Av *EFF/MANN* PL3 17 G4
Wesley Ct *TOR* PL11 23 G1
Wesley La *SALT* PL12 8 D4
Wesley Pl *EFF/MANN* PL3 17 G4
KEY/HAM/PCR PL2 16 B5
Westbourne Rd *EFF/MANN* PL3 17 F4
Westbourne Ter *SALT* PL12 8 D3
Westbury Cl *PLYNW* PL5 10 D2
Westcombe Crs
PLYMST/WEM PL9 32 D2
Westcott Cl *PLYNE* PL6 18 A2
Westcountry Cl
KEY/HAM/PCR PL2 16 B2
Westcroft Rd *PLYNW* PL5 9 H5
West Down Rd
KEY/HAM/PCR PL2 16 D3
West End Ter
MBRK/KGSD PL10 * 30 C3
Westeria Ter *KEY/HAM/PCR* PL2 17 E2
Western Ap *PLY* PL1 3 F3
Western College Rd *PLYE* PL4 17 G4
Western Dr *EFF/MANN* PL3 18 B5
Western Kings *PLY* PL1 24 C5
Western Wood Wy *PLYMP* PL7 21 H4
Westfield *PLYMP* PL7 20 D3
Westfield Av *PLYMST/WEM* PL9 32 C2
Westhays Cl *PLYMST/WEM* PL9 33 F3
Westhead Rd *MBRK/KGSD* PL10 36 C2
West Hl *PLYMST/WEM* PL9 38 G4
West Hill Rd *PLYE* PL4 17 H5
West Hoe Rd *PLY* PL1 2 E5
Westlake Cl *TOR* PL11 22 D1
Westlake Ri *PLYMST/WEM* PL9 38 B3
Westlake Rd *PLYMST/WEM* PL9 38 B3
West Malling Av *PLYNW* PL5 10 A2
Westmoor Cl *PLYMP* PL7 21 G3
Weston Mill Dr *PLYNW* PL5 16 A1
Weston Mill Hl *PLYNW* PL5 10 A5
Weston Mill La *PLYNW* PL5 10 C5
Weston Mill Rd *PLYNW* PL5 10 A5
Weston Park Rd *EFF/MANN* PL3 17 F2
West Park Dr *PLYMP* PL7 21 G4
West Park Hl *PLYMP* PL7 21 F2
West St *MBRK/KGSD* PL10 30 C3
Westwood Av *PLYNE* PL6 6 C5
Wheatridge *PLYMP* PL7 19 H2
Whimple St *PLY* PL1 3 H4
Whin Bank Rd *PLYNW* PL5 11 F4
Whitby Crs *PLYNE* PL6 12 A5
Whitby Rd *PLYNE* PL6 12 A5
Whiteford Rd *EFF/MANN* PL3 17 G3
Whitefriars La *PLYE* PL4 25 H2
Whitehall Dr *PLYMST/WEM* PL9 27 H5
White Lady Rd
PLYMST/WEM PL9 32 D2
Whitleigh Av *PLYNW* PL5 11 G4
Whitleigh Gn *PLYNW* PL5 11 E2
Whitleigh Vls *PLYNW* PL5 11 G4
Whitleigh Wy *PLYNW* PL5 11 E2
Whitsoncross La *PLYNW* PL5 5 E4
Whittington St *EFF/MANN* PL3 24 D1
Widewell La *PLYNE* PL6 6 C4
Widewell Rd *PLYNE* PL6 6 B4
Widey Ct *PLYNE* PL6 11 H5
Widey La *PLYNE* PL6
Widey Vw *EFF/MANN* PL3
Wilcove La *TOR* PL11
Wilderness Rd *PLYE* PL4
Wilkinson Rd *PLYNW* PL5
William Evans Cl *PLYNW* PL5
Willow Cl *EFF/MANN* PL3
Willow Ct *PLYNE* PL6 *
Willow Gn *SALT* PL12 *
Willow Wk *PLYNE* PL6
Wills Cl *PLYNE* PL6
Wilmot Gdns *PLYNW* PL5
Wilson Crs *KEY/HAM/PCR* PL2
Wilton Rd *PLY* PL1
Wilton St *PLY* PL1
Wiltshire Cl *PLYE* PL4
Winchester Gdns *PLYNW* PL5
Windermere Crs *PLYNE* PL6
Windmill Hl *SALT* PL12
Windsor La *SALT* PL12
Windsor Pl *PLY* PL1
Windsor Rd *EFF/MANN* PL3
Wingfield Rd *EFF/MANN* PL3
Wingfield Wy *EFF/MANN* PL3
Winnicott Cl *PLYNE* PL6
Winnow Cl *PLYMST/WEM* PL9
Winsbury Ct *PLYNE* PL6
Winstanley Wk *EFF/MANN* PL3
Winston Av *PLYE* PL4
Winstone La *YLMP* PL8
Woburn Ter *PLYMST/WEM* PL9
Wollaton Gv *PLYNW* PL5
Wolrige Av *PLYMP* PL7
Wolrige Wy *PLYMP* PL7
Wolsdon Pl *PLY* PL1
Wolsdon St *PLY* PL1
Wolseley Cl *KEY/HAM/PCR* PL2
Wolseley Rd *KEY/HAM/PCR* PL2
PLYNW PL5
Wolverwood Cl *PLYMP* PL7
Wolverwood La *PLYMP* PL7
Wombwell Crs
KEY/HAM/PCR PL2
Woodcock Cl
MBRK/KGSD PL10 *
Woodend Rd *PLYNE* PL6
Woodford Av *PLYMP* PL7
Woodford Cl *PLYMP* PL7
Woodford Crs *PLYMP* PL7
Woodford Gn *PLYMP* PL7
Woodford Rd *PLYNE* PL6
Woodhey Rd
KEY/HAM/PCR PL2
Woodland Av
PLYMST/WEM PL9
Woodland Dr *PLYMP* PL7
YLMP PL8
Woodland Rd *PLYMP* PL7
Woodlands *PLYMST/WEM* PL9
Woodlands End *PLYNE* PL6
Woodlands La *PLYNE* PL6
Woodland Ter *PLYE* PL4 *
Woodland Wy *TOR* PL11
Wood Pk *PLYNE* PL6
Woodside *PLYE* PL4
Woodside Av *PLYMST/WEM* PL9
Woodside Ct *PLYMP* PL7
Woodstock Gdns *PLYNW* PL5
Woodview Pk
PLYMST/WEM PL9
Woodville Cl *KEY/HAM/PCR* PL2
Woodville Rd
KEY/HAM/PCR PL2
Woodway *PLYMST/WEM* PL9
Woollcombe Av *PLYMP* PL7
Woolwell Crs *PLYNE* PL6
Woolwell Dr *PLYNE* PL6
Woolwell Rd *PLYNE* PL6
Wordsworth Crs
KEY/HAM/PCR PL2
Wordsworth Rd
KEY/HAM/PCR PL2
Wren Gdns *PLYMP* PL7
Wrens Ga *PLYMST/WEM* PL9
Wright Cl *PLY* PL1
Wycliffe Rd *EFF/MANN* PL3
Wye Gdns *EFF/MANN* PL3
Wykeham Dr
KEY/HAM/PCR PL2
Wyndham La *PLY* PL1
Wyndham Sq *PLY* PL1
Wyndham St East *PLY* PL1
Wyndham St West *PLY* PL1
Wyoming Cl *EFF/MANN* PL3
Wythburn Gdns *PLYNE* PL6

Y

Yardley Gdns *PLYNE* PL6
Yarrow Md *PLYMST/WEM* PL9
Yealmpstone Cl *PLYMP* PL7
Yealmpstone Dr *PLYMP* PL7
Yeats Cl *PLYNW* PL5
Yellow Tor La *SALT* PL12
Yellowtor Rd *SALT* PL12
Yelverton Cl *PLYNW* PL5
Yeo Cl *EFF/MANN* PL3
Yeomans Wy *PLYMP* PL7
Yewdale Gdns *PLYNE* PL6
Yonder St *PLYMST/WEM* PL9
York Pl *KEY/HAM/PCR* PL2
York Rd *PLYNW* PL5
TOR PL11
York St *PLY* PL1
York Ter *KEY/HAM/PCR* PL2

Z

Zion St *PLY* PL1

inema
Y PL1 ... 3 G4
ny House NT
R PL11 ... 14 B4
da Shopping Centre
Y PL1 ... 3 G2
aeum Theatre
Y PL1
n Farm Primary School
YNE PL6 ... 18 C2
d Activity Centre
Y PL1 ... 3 F4
can Glassworks
d Fish Market)
Y PL1 ... 3 K5
can Leisure Centre
YE PL4 ... 26 A3
can Theatre
Y PL1 ... 3 J5
e Barton Primary School
YNW PL5 ... 15 H1
on Business Park
Y/HAM/PCR PL2 ... 17 E2
er Industrial Estate
YNE PL6 ... 6 B2
eigh Down Business Park
YNE PL6 ... 6 D3
eigh Down
Primary School
YNE PL6 ... 6 D3
ap Cornish
Primary School
LT PL12 ... 8 D5
Friars Distillery
Y PL1 ... 3 J5
gton Mill Business Park
YMP PL7 ... 20 D3
agdon Primary School
YMP PL7 ... 20 B2
ckwater Industrial Estate
YMST/WEM PL9 ... 26 C4
on Caravan &
mping Park
YMST/WEM PL9 ... 34 D2
dley Industrial Park
YNE PL6 ... 6 B1
el Primary School
ALT PL12 ... 8 C3
Point Primary School
YNW PL5 ... 9 F5
ton Primary School
ALT PL12 ... 8 A3
ngton Industrial Estate
YNW PL5 ... 10 C5
elot Hotel
Y PL1 ... 3 G5
elle Junior School
OR PL11 ... 23 E1
w Wharf Business Centre
OR PL11 ... 23 G2
eel Industrial Estate
Y PL1 ... 8 A1
edral School of St Mary
Y PL1 ... 2 E2
ral Park Swimming Pool
FF/MANN PL3 ... 17 E4
dlewood J & I School
YMP PL7 ... 21 E4
les Church (Ruin)
LYE PL4 ... 3 J5
cer Primary School
YNE PL6 ... 11 E4
a Fleet Country Club Hotel
ALT PL12 ... 8 D1
stian Mill Business Park
LYNE PL6 ... 11 C3
Business Park
YMST PL3 ... 16 D5
Social Sports Club
EY/HAM/PCR PL2 ... 16 C2
Service Sports Club
YNE PL6 ... 16 D2
ege of St Mark & St John
LYNE PL6 ... 12 C1
ge Road Primary School
EY/HAM/PCR PL2 ... 16 A4
ngs Park Medical Centre
LYMP PL7 ... 17 H3
pton CE Primary School
FF/MANN PL3 ... 18 A3
tinental Ferryport
LY PL1 ... 2 C6
mbe Dean School
LYMST/WEM PL9 ... 33 G1
thorne Hotel
Y PL1 ... 3 G2
wall College Saltash
ALT PL12 ... 8 B4
Hill Trading Estate
LYMP PL7 ... 19 H3
rtlands Special School
LYNE PL6 ... 11 H5
wnhill Fort
LYNE PL6 ... 11 H5
riford Business Park
LYNE PL6 ... 12 A2
riford Hospital
LYNE PL6 ... 12 B3
onport Guildhall
FF/MANN PL3 ... 24 A3
onport High School
or Boys
LY PL1 ... 2 B2
onport High School for Girls
EY/HAM/PCR PL2 ... 17 E3
onport Services RFC
Y PL1 ... 2 A2
smouth Rock
LYMP PL7 ... 20 B5
nham Special School
LYMST/WEM PL9 ... 33 F1
ke Circus
Y PL1 ... 3 J3
ke Hotel
Y PL1 ... 3 G5

Drake Primary School
PLYNW PL5 ... 15 H3
Duke of Cornwall Hotel
PLY PL1 ... 2 E5
Dunstone Primary School
PLYMST/WEM PL9 ... 27 G4
Efford Cemetery
EFF/MANN PL3 ... 18 C3
Efford Clinic
EFF/MANN PL3 ... 18 C3
Efford Crematorium
EFF/MANN PL3 ... 18 C3
Eggbuckland
Community College
PLYMP PL7 ... 18 A1
Eggbuckland Vale
Primary School
PLYMP PL7 ... 18 A1
Elburton Primary School
PLYMST/WEM PL9 ... 28 A5
Elizabethan House
PLY PL1 ... 3 J5
Ernesettle Infant School
PLYNW PL5 ... 10 B2
Erril Retail Park
PLYMP PL7 ... 20 A4
Estover Community College
PLYNE PL6 ... 12 D4
Estover Health Centre
PLYNE PL6 ... 13 E4
Estover Industrial Estate
PLYNE PL6 ... 13 E2
Estover Primary School
PLYNE PL6 ... 12 D4
Faraday Mill Business Park
PLYE PL4 ... 26 B3
Fletewood School
PLYE PL4 ... 3 H1
Ford Primary School
KEY/HAM/PCR PL2 ... 16 B4
Fort Stamford Fitness &
Leisure Centre
PLYMST/WEM PL9 ... 32 A1
Fourlanesend CP School
MBRK/KGSD PL10 ... 31 E4
Freedom Health Centre
PLYE PL4 ... 25 H1
Friary House Surgery
PLYE PL4 ... 25 H2
Fursdon Leisure Centre
PLYNE PL6 ... 12 D3
Gables Hospital
PLYE PL4 ... 28 A1
Glen Park Primary School
PLYMP PL7 ... 21 F4
Glenside Medical Centre
PLYMP PL7 ... 20 C3
Goosewell Primary School
PLYMST/WEM PL9 ... 33 F1
Goschen Centre
(Plymouth College of FE)
KEY/HAM/PCR PL2 ... 16 A4
The Green House Visitor Centre
PLYMST/WEM PL9 ... 26 D2
Grosvenor Park Hotel
PLYE PL4 ... 3 H1
Gwel Avon Business Park
SALT PL12 ... 8 B2
Ham Welfare Clinic
KEY/HAM/PCR PL2 ... 16 C2
Heles School
PLYMP PL7 ... 20 A3
Highfield Primary School
EFF/MANN PL3 ... 18 C4
High Street Primary School
PLY PL1 ... 2 B3
Hillside Special School
PLYMP PL7 ... 10 D2
HMS Cambridge
PLYMST/WEM PL9 ... 38 B5
HMS Raleigh
TOR PL11 ... 22 C2
Holy Cross RC Primary School
PLYE PL4 ... 25 H2
Honicknowle Green
Medical Centre
YLMP PL5 ... 10 D4
Hooe Primary School
PLYMST/WEM PL9 ... 32 B2
Hotel Ibis
PLYNE PL6 ... 19 E2
Hursley Business Park
PLYNE PL6 ... 6 D2
Hyde Park Junior School
EFF/MANN PL3 ... 17 G4
Invicta Hotel
PLY PL1 ... 3 G5
The John Kitto
Community College
PLYNW PL5 ... 10 D5
Keyham Barton RC
Primary School
KEY/HAM/PCR PL2 ... 16 A3
Kings School
EFF/MANN PL3 ... 17 G3
Kitley House Hotel
YLMP PL12 ... 35 F4
Knowle Primary School
PLYNW PL5 ... 10 C2
Laira Green Primary School
EFF/MANN PL3 ... 18 C4
Langage Industrial Estate
PLYMP PL7 ... 21 H4
Langdon Court Hotel
PLYMST/WEM PL9 ... 39 F2
Langley J & I School
PLYMP PL7 ... 6 A5
Learning Warehouse
PLY PL1 ... 3 F5
Leigham Business Park
PLYNE PL6 ... 13 E5
Lipson Vale Primary School
PLYE PL4 ... 18 A5
Lisson Grove Medical Centre
PLYE PL4 ... 17 G5

Longcause Special School
PLYMP PL7 ... 20 D5
Manadon Vale Primary School
PLYNW PL5 ... 17 G1
Marlborough Primary School
PLY PL1 ... 24 A2
Marsh Mills Retail Park
PLYNE PL6 ... 19 E2
Mary Deans CE Primary School
PLYNW PL5 ... 5 E4
Mary Newman's Cottage
SALT PL12 ... 9 E4
Mayflower Sailing Club
PLY PL1 ... 3 K6
Mayflower Sports Centre
KEY/HAM/PCR PL2 ... 17 E4
Mayflower Steps Monument
PLY PL1 ... 3 K6
Megabowl
PLYE PL4 ... 25 H3
PLYMP PL7 ... 19 H4
Merchant's House Museum
PLY PL1 ... 3 H5
Methodist Central Hall
PLY PL1 ... 3 H3
Millbrook CE
Primary School
MBRK/KGSD PL10 ... 30 C2
Mill Ford Special School
PLYNW PL5 ... 10 B2
Montpelier J & I School
KEY/HAM/PCR PL2 ... 16 D3
Moorlands Trading Estate
SALT PL12 ... 8 A2
The Mount Batten Sailing &
Watersport Centre
PLYMST/WEM PL9 ... 25 H5
Mount Edgcumbe House &
Country Park
MBRK/KGSD PL10 ... 31 H2
Mount Street Primary School
PLYE PL4 ... 3 J1
Mount Tamar Special School
PLYNW PL5 ... 10 A4
Mount Wise Primary School
PLY PL1 ... 24 A3
National Marine Aquarium
PLY PL1 ... 3 K6
New Continental Hotel
PLY PL1 ... 3 F4
Newnham Industrial Estate
PLYMP PL7 ... 20 D3
North Prospect
Community School
KEY/HAM/PCR PL2 ... 16 C2
North Quay
PLY PL1 ... 2 D5
Notre Dame RC School
PLYNE PL6 ... 12 A1
Novotel
PLYNE PL6 ... 19 F3
Nuffield Hospital
PLYNE PL6 ... 12 B2
Old Custom House (RNLI)
PLY PL1 ... 2 E7
The Old Mill NT
PLYMST/WEM PL9 ... 39 H5
Old Priory Junior School
PLYMP PL7 ... 20 B4
Oreston Community
Primary School
PLYMST/WEM PL9 ... 26 C5
Pannier Market
PLY PL1 ... 3 F5
Parkside Community
Technology College
KEY/HAM/PCR PL2 ... 24 A1
Parkside
Comprehensive School
PLY PL1 ... 24 A1
The Parkway Industrial
Estate
PLYNE PL6 ... 19 F2
Pavilions Conference &
Leisure Centre
PLY PL1 ... 2 E4
Pennycross Primary School
KEY/HAM/PCR PL2 ... 17 E1
Phoenix Business Park
PLYNE PL6 ... 13 F2
Pilgrim Primary School
PLY PL1 ... 3 F2
Plaistow Hill Infant School
PLYNW PL5 ... 10 A4
The Plantings School
EFF/MANN PL3 ... 17 G3
Plymouth Albion RFC
KEY/HAM/PCR PL2 ... 16 D2
Plymouth Argyle FC
(Home Park)
KEY/HAM/PCR PL2 ... 17 E4
Plymouth Arts Centre
PLYE PL4 ... 3 J4
The Plymouth Business Park
PLYNE PL6 ... 11 H2
Plymouth City Airport
PLYNE PL6 ... 12 C1
Plymouth City Museum
& Art Gallery
PLYE PL4 ... 3 H2
Plymouth College
PLYE PL4 ... 17 G5
Plymouth College of
Art & Design
PLY PL1 ... 3 J2
Plymouth College of Further
Education
PLYE PL4 ... 2 A2
Plymouth College
Preparatory School
EFF/MANN PL3 ... 17 H3
Plymouth Discovery Centre
EFF/MANN PL3 ... 19 F4
Plymouth Dome
PLY PL1 ... 3 C6

Plymouth Girls High School
PLYE PL4 ... 25 G1
Plymouth International
Business Park
PLYNE PL6 ... 12 A3
Plymouth Marine Laboratory
PLY PL1 ... 3 F6
Plymouth Ski Centre
PLYNE PL6 ... 19 E2
Plymouth Sports Club
KEY/HAM/PCR PL2 ... 17 E3
Plympton Health Centre
PLYMP PL7 ... 20 C4
Plympton Hospital
PLYMP PL7 ... 20 B4
Plympton Swimming Pool
PLYMP PL7 ... 20 B4
Plymstock Clinic
PLYMST/WEM PL9 ... 27 F5
Plymstock School
PLYMST/WEM PL9 ... 27 F4
Plym Valley Railway
PLYMP PL7 ... 19 G1
Plym View Primary School
EFF/MANN PL3 ... 18 D3
Pomphlett Farm
Industrial Estate
PLYMST/WEM PL9 ... 27 E3
Pomphlett Primary School
PLYMST/WEM PL9 ... 27 E4
Premier Travel Inn
EFF/MANN PL3 ... 19 E3
PLYE PL4 ... 25 H3
Prince Rock Primary School
PLYE PL4 ... 26 B2
Racquets Sports Club
TOR PL11 ... 23 F1
RC Cathedral
PLY PL1 ... 2 E2
Recreation Road
Industrial Estate
KEY/HAM/PCR PL2 ... 17 E2
Ridgeway School
PLYMP PL7 ... 20 C4
Riverside Business Park
PLYNW PL5 ... 24 A1
Riverside Caravan Park
PLYNE PL6 ... 19 F2
Royal Citadel
PLY PL1 ... 3 J6
Royal Eye Infirmary
PLYE PL4 ... 17 G5
Royal Naval Gunnery School
PLYMST/WEM PL9 ... 38 B5
The Royal Plymouth
Corinthian Yacht Club
PLY PL1 ... 3 J7
St Andrews CE
Primary School
PLY PL1 ... 3 F5
St Andrews Church &
Prysten House
PLY PL1 ... 3 H4
St. Barnabas Hospital
SALT PL12 ... 8 D4
St Boniface RC College
PLYNW PL5 ... 11 G5
St Budeaux Foundation
Junior School
PLYNW PL5 ... 10 B4
St. Budeaux Health Centre
PLYNW PL5 ... 9 H5
St. Dunstans Abbey School
PLY PL1 ... 2 C3
St Edwards CE Primary School
PLYNE PL6 ... 12 C5
St Georges CE Primary School
PLY PL1 ... 2 C7
St Josephs RC Primary School
PLY PL1 ... 24 B2
St Mary CE Infant School
PLYMP PL7 ... 20 A4
St Marys School
PLYMP PL7 ... 20 B4
St Marys Voluntary
Primary School
PLYE PL8 ... 35 E2
St Maurice Primary School
PLYMP PL7 ... 28 C1
St Pauls RC Primary School
PLYNW PL5 ... 9 G5
St Peters CE Primary School
PLY PL1 ... 2 E3
St Peters RC Primary School
PLYNW PL5 ... 10 D1
St Stephens Primary School
SALT PL12 ... 8 A1
Salisbury Road J & I School
PLYE PL4 ... 25 H2
Salisbury Road Surgery
PLYE PL4 ... 25 H1
Saltash Business Park
SALT PL12 ... 8 A2
Saltash Community School
SALT PL12 ... 8 C5
Saltash Health Centre
SALT PL12 ... 8 C3
Saltash Industrial Estate
SALT PL12 ... 8 B1
Saltash RFC
SALT PL12 ... 8 A2
Saltram House NT
PLYMP PL7 ... 19 G5
Seaton Business Park
PLYNE PL6 ... 12 A3
Seaton Swimming Pool
PLYNE PL6 ... 12 A3
Sir John Hurt
Community College
PLYNW PL5 ... 11 F2
Smeaton's Tower
PLY PL1 ... 3 H6
South Trelawny
Primary School
KEY/HAM/PCR PL2 ... 16 C1

Southway Community College
PLYNW PL6 ... 5 G5
Southway Primary School
PLYNW PL6 ... 5 G5
Staddon Heights Golf Club
PLYMST/WEM PL9 ... 32 B3
Stoke Damerel Business Centre
EFF/MANN PL3 ... 16 C5
Stoke Damerel
Community College
EFF/MANN PL3 ... 16 D5
Stoke Damerel Primary School
PLY PL1 ... 24 B1
Stuart Road Primary School
PLY PL1 ... 24 D1
Sugarmill Business Park
PLYMST/WEM PL9 ... 26 C3
TA Centre
PLY PL1 ... 2 E6
Tamar Science Park
PLYNE PL6 ... 12 C2
Tamarside Community College
PLYNW PL5 ... 10 A5
Tamar View Industrial Estate
SALT PL12 ... 8 B1
Tamerton Vale Primary School
PLYNE PL6 ... 5 E5
Tannery Business Park
PLYE PL4 ... 3 K1
Theatre Royal
PLY PL1 ... 3 G4
Thornbury Primary School
PLYNE PL6 ... 12 D2
Tinside Lido
PLY PL1 ... 3 H7
Torpoint Community School
TOR PL11 ... 14 C3
Torpoint Infant School
TOR PL11 ... 23 F1
Travelodge
PLY PL1 ... 3 F4
SALT PL12 ... 8 A1
Trengweath School
EFF/MANN PL3 ... 17 G3
Trevol Business Park
TOR PL11 ... 22 C1
University of Plymouth
PLYE PL4 ... 3 H5
PLYE PL4 ... 3 H1
University of Plymouth
(Babbage Building)
PLYE PL4 ... 3 H1
University of Plymouth
(Brunel Laboratories)
PLYE PL4 ... 3 H1
University of Plymouth
(Cookworthy Building)
PLYE PL4 ... 3 J2
University of Plymouth
(Davy Building)
PLYE PL4 ... 3 H2
University of Plymouth
(Halls of Residence)
PLYE PL4 ... 3 J2
University of Plymouth
(Library)
PLYE PL4 ... 3 H1
University of Plymouth
(Pitts Memorial Hall)
PLYE PL4 ... 3 J2
University of Plymouth
(Robbins Hall &
Conference Centre)
PLYE PL4 ... 3 J2
University of Plymouth
(Sherwell Centre)
PLYE PL4 ... 3 J1
Victoria Court Hotel
PLY PL1 ... 25 F1
Victoria Road Primary School
PLYNW PL5 ... 9 H5
VUE Cinema
PLYE PL4 ... 25 H3
Walkham Business Park
PLYNW PL5 ... 10 D5
Wallsend Industrial Estate
PLYE PL4 ... 26 A4
Wembury Marine Centre
PLYMST/WEM PL9 ... 39 F5
Wembury Primary School
PLYMST/WEM PL9 ... 39 H2
Weston Mill Crematorium
KEY/HAM/PCR PL2 ... 16 B2
Weston Mill Primary School
KEY/HAM/PCR PL2 ... 16 A2
West Park Primary School
PLYNW PL5 ... 10 C4
West Wharf
PLY PL1 ... 2 C6
Whitleigh Primary School
PLYNW PL5 ... 11 F2
Widewell Primary School
PLYNE PL6 ... 6 B4
Widey Court Primary School
PLYNE PL6 ... 11 H5
Wolston Street School
PLY PL1 ... 2 E2
Wolseley Business Park
KEY/HAM/PCR PL2 ... 16 C4
Woodfield Primary School
PLYNW PL5 ... 11 E1
Woodford J & I School
PLYMP PL7 ... 19 H3
Woodland Garden
TOR PL11 ... 14 B4
Woodlands Special School
PLYNE PL6 ... 10 D2
Woolwell Medical Centre
PLYNE PL6 ... 6 D3
Yealmpstone Farm
Primary School
PLYMP PL7 ... 29 E1

48 Acknowledgements

The Post Office is a registered trademark of Post Office Ltd. in the UK and other countries.

Schools address data provided by Education Direct.

Petrol station information supplied by Johnsons

One-way street data provided by © Tele Atlas N.V. Tele Atlas

Garden centre information provided by

Garden Centre Association   Britains best garden centres

Wyevale Garden Centres

The statement on the front cover of this atlas is sourced, selected and quoted from a reader comment and feedback form received in 2004

AA **Street by Street** QUESTIONNAIRE

Dear Atlas User
Your comments, opinions and recommendations are very important to us.
So please help us to improve our street atlases by taking a few minutes
to complete this simple questionnaire.

You do not need a stamp (unless posted outside the UK). If you do not want to remove
this page from your street atlas, then photocopy it or write your answers on a plain sheet
of paper.

Send to: The Editor, AA Street by Street, FREEPOST SCE 4598,
Basingstoke RG21 4GY

ABOUT THE ATLAS...

Which city/town/county did you buy?

_____

Are there any features of the atlas or mapping that you find particularly useful?

_____
_____
_____

Is there anything we could have done better?

_____
_____
_____

Why did you choose an AA Street by Street atlas?

_____
_____
_____

Did it meet your expectations?

Exceeded ☐   **Met all** ☐   **Met most** ☐   **Fell below** ☐

Please give your reasons

_____
_____
_____
_____

Where did you buy it?

For what purpose? (please tick all applicable)

To use in your own local area ☐   **To use on business or at work** ☐

Visiting a strange place ☐   **In the car** ☐   **On foot** ☐

Other (please state)

LOCAL KNOWLEDGE...

Local knowledge is invaluable. Whilst every attempt has been made to make the information contained in this atlas as accurate as possible, should you notice any inaccuracies, please detail them below (if necessary, use a blank piece of paper) or e-mail us at *streetbystreet@theAA.com*

ABOUT YOU...

Name (Mr/Mrs/Ms)

Address

Postcode

Daytime tel no   **Mobile tel no**

E-mail address

Please only give us your e-mail address and mobile phone number if you wish to hear from us about other products and services from the AA and partners by e-mail or text or mms.

Which age group are you in?

Under 25 ☐   **25-34** ☐   **35-44** ☐   **45-54** ☐   **55-64** ☐   **65+** ☐

Are you an AA member?   **YES** ☐   **NO** ☐

Do you have Internet access?   **YES** ☐   **NO** ☐

The information we hold about you will be used to provide the product(s) and service(s) requested and for identification, account administration, analysis, and fraud/loss prevention purposes. More details about how that information is used is in our Privacy Statement, which you will find under the heading "Personal information" in our Terms and Conditions and on our website. Copies are available from us by post, by contacting our Data Protection Manager at AA, Fanum House, Basing View, Basingstoke, Hampshire, RG21 4EA.
We may want to contact you about other products and services provided by us or our partners but please tick the box if you DO NOT wish to hear about such products and services from us by mail or telephone. ☐

Thank you for taking the time to complete this questionnaire. Please send it to us as soon as possible, and remember, you do not need a stamp (unless posted outside the UK).   ML110y

Discover
Britain
with AA travel guides.